The International Committee of the Red Cross

The International Committee of the Red Cross (ICRC) has a complex position in international relations, being the guardian of international humanitarian law but often acting discretely to advance human dignity. Treated by most governments as if it were an inter-governmental organization, the ICRC is a non-governmental organization, all-Swiss at the top, and it is given rights and duties in the 1949 Geneva Conventions for Victims of War.

Written by two formidable experts in the field, this book analyzes international humanitarian action as practised by the ICRC, explaining its history and structure as well as examining contemporary field experience and broad diplomatic initiatives related to its principal tasks. Such tasks include:

- ensuring that detention conditions are humane for those imprisoned becasue of political conflict or war;
- providing material and moral relief in conflict;
- promoting development of the humanitarian aspects of the laws of war;
- improving the unity and effectiveness of the movement.

Fully updated throughout, the new edition includes brand new material on:

- armed actors who do not accept humanitarian restrictions on their actions, including expanded coverage of the Islamic State (ISIL, ISIS), Al Shabab, and Boko Haram, among others;
- the Syrian internationalized civil war;
- the issue of drone strikes and targeted killings, and the continuing push for regulation of what is called cyber war;
- the question of the field of application of international humanitarian law (what is the battlefield?), particularly when states declare war on terrorist groups operating inside other states;
- regulation of new weapons and new uses of old weapons.

David P. Forsythe is Emeritus University Professor and Charles J. Mach Distinguished Professor of Political Science at the University of Nebraska–Lincoln, USA

Barbara Ann J. Rieffer-Flanagan is Professor of Political Science at Central Washington University, USA.

Global Institutions

Edited by Thomas G. Weiss
The CUNY Graduate Center, New York, USA
and Rorden Wilkinson
University of Sussex, Brighton, UK

About the series

The "Global Institutions Series" provides cutting-edge books about many aspects of what we know as "global governance." It emerges from our shared frustrations with the state of available knowledge—electronic and print-wise, for research and teaching—in the area. The series is designed as a resource for those interested in exploring issues of international organization and global governance. And since the first volumes appeared in 2005, we have taken significant strides toward filling conceptual gaps.

The series consists of three related "streams" distinguished by their blue, red, and green covers. The blue volumes, comprising the majority of the books in the series, provide user-friendly and short (usually no more than 50,000 words) but authoritative guides to major global and regional organizations, as well as key issues in the global governance of security, the environment, human rights, poverty, and humanitarian action among others. The books with red covers are designed to present original research and serve as extended and more specialized treatments of issues pertinent for advancing understanding about global governance. And the volumes with green covers—the most recent departure in the series—are comprehensive and accessible accounts of the major theoretical approaches to global governance and international organization.

The books in each of the streams are written by experts in the field, ranging from the most senior and respected authors to first-rate scholars at the beginning of their careers. In combination, the three components of the series—blue, red, and green—serve as key resources for faculty, students, and practitioners alike. The works in the blue and green streams have value as core and complementary readings in courses on, among other things, international organization, global governance, international law, international relations, and international political economy; the red volumes allow further reflection and investigation in these and related areas.

The books in the series also provide a segue to the foundation volume that offers the most comprehensive textbook treatment available dealing with all the major issues, approaches, institutions, and actors in contemporary global governance—our edited work *International Organization and Global Governance* (2014)—a volume to which many of the authors in the series have contributed essays.

Understanding global governance—past, present, and future—is far from a finished journey. The books in this series nonetheless represent significant steps toward a better way of conceiving contemporary problems and issues as well as, hopefully, doing something to improve world order. We value the feedback from our readers and their role in helping shape the on-going development of the series.

A complete list of titles appears at the end of this book. The most recent titles in the series are:

The International Committee of the Red Cross

A neutral humanitarian actor

Second edition

**David P. Forsythe and
Barbara Ann J. Rieffer-Flanagan**

Routledge
Taylor & Francis Group

LONDON AND NEW YORK

Second edition published 2016
by Routledge
2 Park Square, Milton Park, Abingdon, Oxon OX14 4RN

and by Routledge
711 Third Avenue, New York, NY 10017

Routledge is an imprint of the Taylor & Francis Group, an informa business

© 2016 David P. Forsythe and Barbara Ann J. Rieffer-Flanagan

The right of David P. Forsythe and Barbara Ann J. Rieffer-Flanagan to be identified as authors of the editorial material, and of the individual authors as authors of their contributions, has been asserted by them in accordance with sections 77 and 78 of the Copyright, Designs and Patents Act 1988.

[First edition published by Routledge 2007]

British Library Cataloguing in Publication Data
A catalogue record for this book is available from the British Library

Library of Congress Cataloging in Publication Data
Names: Forsythe, David P., 1941- author. | Rieffer-Flanagan, Barbara Ann J., author.
 Title: The International Committee of the Red Cross : a neutral humanitarian actor / David P. Forsythe and Barbara Ann J. Rieffer-Flanagan.
 Description: Abingdon, Oxon ; New York, NY : Routledge, 2016. | Series: Routledge global institutions series | Earlier edition: 2007. | Includes bibliographical references and index.
 Identifiers: LCCN 2015046318| ISBN 9781138185524 (hardback) | ISBN 9781138185548 (pbk.) | ISBN 9781315644448 (ebook)
 Subjects: LCSH: International Committee of the Red Cross. | Humanitarian assistance. | International relief.
 Classification: LCC HV568 .F673 2016 | DDC 361.7/72–dc23
 LC record available at http://lccn.loc.gov/2015046318

ISBN: 978-1-138-18552-4 (hbk)
ISBN: 978-1-138-18554-8 (pbk)
ISBN: 978-1-31564-444-8 (ebk)

Typeset in Times New Roman
by Taylor & Francis Books

For Jacques Moreillon and Rosemary Rieffer

Contents

List of illustrations

Tables

Boxes

Acknowledgement

We are grateful to a number of persons at the ICRC in Geneva who interacted with us over considerable time, answering our questions and further explaining a number of ICRC dilemmas and policies. The latest of these meetings occurred in December 2015.

In addition, several persons read earlier drafts and even helped us edit the final versions. In this regard we would like to thank especially Amanda Baskin and Kristan Hawkins.

Dave P. Forsythe would like to thank particularly Jacques Moreillon, who for over forty years has been not only a professional colleague interested in humanitarian affairs but also a warm friend.

Barbara Ann J. Rieffer-Flanagan would like to thank particularly Rosemary Rieffer for her support and encouragement over the years.

Tom Weiss was an encouraging series editor.

List of abbreviations

ACLU	American Civil Liberties Union
AI	Amnesty International
ARC	American Red Cross
AP	Additional Protocol
BBC	British Broadcasting Corporation
CIA	Central Intelligence Agency
CNN	Cable Network News
ECHO	European Communities Humanitarian Office
GC	Geneva Convention
Gitmo	US detention facility, Guantanamo Bay, Cuba
ICRC	International Committee of the Red Cross
ICTY	International Criminal Tribunal for former Yugoslavia
ICVA	International Council of Voluntary Agencies
IGOs	Inter-governmental Organizations
IHL	International Humanitarian Law
IL	International Law
ISIS/ISIL	The Islamic State
JAG	Judge Advocate General (US)
JCA	Joint Church Aid (Nigerian Civil War)
MDA	Magen David Adom (Israeli RC society)
MSF	Doctors Without Borders (Médecins Sans Frontières)
NATO	North Atlantic Treaty Organization
NGO	Non-governmental Organization
PBS	Public Broadcasting Service (US)
PLO	Palestinian Liberation Organization
POW	Prisoner of War
RC	Red Cross or Red Crescent or Red Crystal
UN	United Nations
UNHCR	United Nations High Commissioner for Refugees
UNICEF	United Nations Children's Fund

UNOSOM	United Nations Operation in Somalia
UNPROFOR	United Nations Protection Force (Balkans
USAID	United States Agency for International Development
WFP	World Food Programme (UN)
WHO	World Health Organization (UN)
WWI	World War I
WWII	World War II

Introduction

In 1859 the Swiss businessman Henry Dunant happened across the terrible Battle of Solferino, in what is now northern Italy, and was shocked to find the wounded soldiers there entirely uncared for. The European powers fighting this battle, the French and Austrians, provided more veterinarians to care for horses than medical personnel to care for soldiers.[1] Dunant organized medical relief on the spot with the help of local personnel, mostly women, and saw to it that soldiers on both sides were cared for. He was so profoundly affected by what he had witnessed at Solferino that upon returning to Geneva, Dunant began a campaign to develop a network of private aid societies.[2] In doing so, his goal was to organize volunteers to care for those injured in war. In 1863, a group of public-minded Genevans, inspired by Dunant's work, built an organization that eventually became the International Committee of the Red Cross (ICRC). In turn, the ICRC became the founding agent for the International Red Cross Movement.[3]

By 2015 there were over 185 national RC societies (e.g. the American Red Cross, the Iraqi Red Crescent) in the Movement.[4] These national RC societies have to be recognized by the ICRC. This occurs when certain conditions are met. For example, an RC society must be accepted by the government of that state; there can be only one such official aid society in each state; the society has to use an emblem recognized as a neutral emblem by states meeting in a diplomatic conference (either a Red Cross, a Red Crescent, or a Red Crystal), and so on. Furthermore, these national societies have their own union, which is called the Federation. All of these units of the Movement, plus state parties to the Geneva Conventions and Protocols for Victims of War, meet periodically in a Conference of the Movement.

At the center of all this remains the ICRC, which, legally speaking, is a private, self-governing Swiss association. Its top policy-making body is an assembly of Swiss citizens numbering no more than 25. The Assembly does not take binding instructions from the Conference, the Federation, or any other body. The ICRC is also independent from the United Nations, although since 1990 it has had observer status in the UN General Assembly and sometimes works closely with UN organs and agencies in practical matters. The ICRC is a rather unique non-governmental organization (NGO). It, unlike most other NGOs, has important and specialized rights and duties in public international law. The general focus of the ICRC has remained consistent from 1863 until today. It has chosen to focus on the protection of human dignity in conflicts. Thus, it started in 1863 with a concern for the wounded combatants in international war.[5] By World War I it firmly added a concern for both civilians and captured combatants in international war. At almost the same time, in about 1920 in both Hungary and the new Soviet Union, it took action for detainees in exceptional situations not recognized as war. These latter victims of conflicts are sometimes referred to as security or political prisoners. Along the way the ICRC made clear that it was also interested in internal or civil wars—as in the Balkans in the 1870s, then part of the Ottoman Empire, and as in the Spanish Civil War of the 1930s. So, in terms of situations, the ICRC focuses on armed conflict (both international and internal), and internal troubles and tensions where there is exceptional detention and/or civilian need.

The organization has played a number of roles throughout its existence. The ICRC has become an actor "on the ground" which seeks to protect the dignity of individuals, both combatants and civilians, in times of conflict. It has also helped to create and develop the legal framework which guides the actions of itself and others. At first the ICRC did not see itself engaging in field action but rather helping to organize the activities of national aid societies. Once it became an actor "in the field," it can be said that over time ICRC activities to protect the dignity of persons often came first and legal codification followed. For example, during World War I, the ICRC showed concern for prisoners of war though they were not part of the mandate of the 1864 or 1906 Geneva Conventions. Precise legal rules for the care of POWs were later developed in the 1929 Geneva Convention. Thus the ICRC is both an actor on the ground and an organization that helps to develop international humanitarian law (IHL)—the law to protect human dignity in war. That law often reflects its field work.

In terms of victims, the ICRC is concerned with combatants who are out of the fight because of wounds, sickness, or detention; and with civilians in need because of "political" events. In these "man-made" or "political" disasters, the ICRC is supposed to be the lead actor for the Movement when an international response is required. That is to say, the ICRC is supposed to be the chief coordinating agent for the rest of the Movement in wars and domestic unrest.

The national societies and the Federation (and Conference) may become involved in natural and industrial/technological disasters such as hurricanes and factory explosions. Normally the ICRC is not directly involved in these problems, but in some instances the organization may be asked to lend its assistance. Helping to trace missing persons on the US Gulf Coast after Hurricane Katrina in 2005, at the request of the American RC, is one example of such involvement. The ICRC retains its overall lead status when a natural or industrial disaster occurs in a state where some kind of war or domestic unrest is also occurring. In general, however, emergency action in peacetime is the domain of the national societies and the Federation. The ICRC acts primarily with regard to conflict situations.

The domain of the ICRC in these conflicts is the realm of humanitarian protection writ large. As a humanitarian actor, the ICRC seeks to be independent, neutral, and impartial. The organization tries to be independent from governments and inter-governmental organizations like the United Nations. It attempts to be neutral in power struggles, by not favoring either side in a conflict whether by motivation or major impact. It endeavors to be impartial by treating similar human suffering in similar ways. That is, a war victim in the Sudan or Democratic Republic of Congo should receive the same attention as a war victim in Iraq or Afghanistan. As the slogan devised by the ICRC's eminent figure Jean Pictet has it, "blood has the same color everywhere."

Humanitarian protection generally means three things: developing a legal framework (humanitarian law and human rights law) that formalizes the minimal standards required for human dignity in conflicts; supervising the conditions of detention in war and exceptional national instability; and providing for the basic needs of the civilian population in these same situations—including during an occupation after war. This latter role of helping civilians means not only helping to provide food, water, shelter, and health care; but also the tracing of missing persons, restoration of family contacts, and other help for civilians in various conditions of distress (e.g. reintegrating child soldiers into civil society).

At the time of writing, the ICRC operated on a yearly budget of about $1.4 billion, over 90 percent of which was voluntarily provided by governments and inter-governmental organizations—mainly Western ones. There are no mandatory state dues. States can pledge support for the Geneva Conventions and Protocols, constituting the core of modern IHL, but not pay any set amount to the ICRC. The same is true for national Red Cross or Red Crescent societies. The ICRC budget was used to employ about 950 persons at its headquarters in Geneva and another 1,600 professional staff around the world. It also hired about 11,500 persons locally in its more than 200 different offices. These offices were organized into various national and regional delegations. From the early 1990s its professional staff was internationalized; only the top body, the Assembly, was permanently all-Swiss. The all-Swiss Assembly, an accident of history, was retained primarily because it guaranteed that in a conflict—assuming the neutral Swiss state was not involved—no one from a fighting party would have any representative on the Assembly. Thus the nature of the Assembly is widely taken as an institutional guarantee of initial neutrality.

The ICRC, despite its origins as a small Swiss private association, has developed into an agency with global reach that is treated by governments as if it were an inter-governmental organization with an impressive international reputation. This reputation developed as a result of its activities in various conflicts throughout the twentieth century. Its accomplishments have been recognized by others. The ICRC has won two Nobel peace prizes—in 1917 and 1944. In 1963 it shared that prize with the RC Federation. Back in 1907, because of his work which served as the precursor to the ICRC, Henry Dunant shared the very first Nobel peace prize with the French pacifist Frederick Passy. No other organization has been so honored so many times. This is somewhat ironic, because the ICRC takes no stand on peace and war in particular conflicts. As a matter of principle, of course it is in favor of peace and opposed to the carnage of war. However, its concern is with limiting the process of war so as to protect the dignity of persons to the greatest extent possible, not with trying to specify and distinguish just wars from unjust wars, or legal wars of self-defense from illegal wars of aggression. In its daily work, it takes the possibility of war as an unpleasant reality and tries to mitigate the suffering of victims.

Despite its Nobel peace prizes and broad recognition for distinguished service over time, the ICRC is not free from controversy.[6] Skeptics criticize the ICRC in general for being naïve and idealistic; they argue that it is silly to attempt to moderate war. Supposedly no fighting party will accept limitations on violence if it means defeat. On the other hand, some pacifists criticize the organization for actually perpetuating war by making it more tolerable. In their view, if the ICRC had not helped develop IHL to protect various victims, war would be more clearly seen as a horrible thing and eventually done away with. Less sweeping critiques also exist—namely, that the organization in its history has not been as independent, neutral, and impartial as often pictured. Some say the ICRC has been linked too closely to the Swiss government (this was especially detrimental during World War II). The ICRC itself has accepted that it was not as dynamic as it should have been in trying to protect European Jews and others victimized by the Nazis, in part because of pressures from persons in the Swiss state. Another critique is that the ICRC has reflected Swiss biases, and hence was at times less than fully committed to treating non-whites, women, and non-Christians as equals. Still other critics argue that the organization tilted toward the West during the Cold War, or that it showed more interest in European victims than others in the 1930s and 1940s. Still others believe the ICRC is too cautious, too discreet, too reluctant to publicly speak out against violations of IHL and other affronts to human dignity—either because of shying away from public controversy or of not wanting to offend its major donors (which are Western states, and above all, the United States).

Ultimately one can raise the question of whether the ICRC has become passé because many other actors in international relations now deal with human dignity in conflicts. On the other hand, one may inquire whether the organization has maintained a unique and valuable role that has not been eclipsed by others, whether they be intergovernmental organizations like the United Nations or NATO, or non-governmental organizations like Amnesty International or Doctors Without Borders.

This short book provides an analytical overview of the ICRC and, in so doing, grounds for dealing with these sorts of controversies and questions. We begin with a discussion of the origins and evolution of the ICRC. Chapter 1 describes the unlikely origins of this humanitarian organization in Geneva, Switzerland, and follows its history to the Cold War. In this chapter we look in some detail at the activities of the ICRC during World War I and II and in various conflicts thereafter. Chapter 2 looks at the structure of the organization, including the office of the President, the Assembly, and the professional staff of the ICRC. In setting out the composition of the ICRC we explain how policy decisions are made. The next few chapters detail some of the significant functions of the ICRC, including the legal development of IHL, relief operations, and detention visits. The last chapter analyzes some of the emerging issues that the ICRC will be forced to deal with.

We look specifically at the war on terrorism that arose after 9/11 and how the ICRC has adjusted to this new international (dis)order.

Notes

1 Francois Bugnion, *The International Committee of the Red Cross and the Protection of War Victims* (Geneva, Switzerland: ICRC, 2003).
2 Henry Dunant, *A Memory of Solferino* (Geneva, Switzerland: Fick, 1862).
3 Because there are now three emblems recognized by states as neutral symbols in war—the Red Cross, the Red Crescent, and from 2005/6 the Red Crystal—we refer to the RC Movement and the RC national aid societies.
4 "The Movement" refers to the network of all RC bodies and used to be called the International Red Cross.
5 War is used as a synonym for what lawyers call "armed conflict".
6 See further David P. Forsythe, *The Humanitarians: The International Committee of the Red Cross* (Cambridge: Cambridge University Press, 2005).

1   Historical development

- The birth and early years of the ICRC
- Development of the organization
- The first major challenges
- Expanding international humanitarian law
- Decolonization and national liberation
- Challenges in the Western Hemisphere
- Organizational changes
- Conclusions

The birth and early years of the ICRC   *Origins in 1859*

As discussed in the Introduction, the ICRC has its origins in the Battle of Solferino in 1859. This battle, which occurred in present-day northern Italy, was part of the Franco-Austrian War. It was after witnessing the bloodshed at the Battle of Solferino, and the lack of medical attention for those wounded, that Henry Dunant felt compelled to work toward a remedy for this lack of care. Dunant, writing his account of the battle in *A Memory of Solferino* (1862), described the battlefield as "a disaster from the point of view of humanity."[1] On the battleground lay corpses amid pools of blood and over 23,000 wounded.[2] Dunant was appalled to learn that there were few doctors or medical services available for badly wounded soldiers.

In response to the atrocious conditions of the injured soldiers at Solferino, Dunant began a drive to assist the wounded in war via private societies. In his words, "Would it not be possible to create societies in every European country whose aim would be to assure that prompt and devoted care is given to those wounded in battle?"[3] These ideas would eventually lead to the creation of the International Committee of the Red Cross, the International RC Movement, and the development of the Geneva Conventions for Victims of War. Dunant was not alone in his concerns for the vulnerable in war, nor was he the first to consider the issue. Jean-Jacques Rousseau, a philosopher also from Geneva, wrote in the eighteenth century that states declare war against one another, not against individual soldiers. Therefore, when soldiers stopped fighting because of injury or surrender, they cease to be legitimate targets and should be treated with respect.[4] Florence Nightingale and Clara Barton were also concerned for the welfare of the injured in war and offered medical assistance to those in need (although some of their activities were unknown to Dunant in the 1860s). In addition, Francis Lieber, also Swiss, developed a set of rules to limit war during the American Civil War of 1861–1865.

The ten years after Dunant visited the Battlefield of Solferino were a crucial time in the development of what became the ICRC. When Dunant returned from Italy he began a campaign for the creation of private aid societies to assist those individuals wounded in combat. He envisioned the creation of national organizations in countries throughout Europe. To further this goal he distributed *A Memory of Solferino*. This manuscript was well received throughout Europe due to Dunant's vivid description of the horrors of war. Many of the pious and philanthropic individuals who lived in Geneva in the 1860s were drawn to Dunant's vision. Genevans such as General Henri Dufour, attorney Gustave Moynier, Dr. Louis Appia, and Dr. Théodore Maunoir took Dunant's work seriously and, with Dunant, created the International Committee for the Relief to the Wounded in Situations of War.[5] These individuals, especially Moynier with his organizational abilities, would have a profound impact on the direction of the organization and of humanitarian protection. Moynier was active in the organization for over 40 years and was president from 1864 to 1910. Appia observed various wars, including Schleswig-Holstein (1864) and wrote numerous commentaries and reports for Geneva. Dufour was also influential as a military leader. His humanitarian orders (protection for women, children, and the wounded) in the Swiss civil war (1847) put many of the ideas into practice that Dunant was to popularize slightly more than ten years later.

The first significant step to implementing Dunant's vision was initiating a conference in October 1863 of private individuals and some government officials from various Western states, to see how receptive they were to private assistance to those wounded in war. This was followed by a conference of states, with the help of the Swiss government, to codify humanitarian principles. The goal for men such as Dufour and Dunant was to humanize and civilize war. States had more pragmatic motivations for their interest in aiding wounded soldiers. With uel**ig**iou

technology improving, countries were confronted by weapons that could do greater damage (dum-dum bullets) as well as improvements in the transmission of information from battlefields (telegraph). Hence, soldiers who fought for their countries were suffering more gruesome wounds and citizens at home learned about it more quickly. Thus, national leaders sought to limit domestic criticism by helping their wounded nationals.[6] And therein lies an enduring aspect of the RC Movement: state pragmatism and self-interest alongside humanitarian goals.

It is worth noting the role religious motivation played in the development of the ICRC and humanitarian principles of war. Dunant's powerful religious drive led him to believe he had been chosen to accomplish a divine mission. While others were not as convinced of divine intervention, they too saw the role of Christian devotion to the less fortunate as an important element in humanitarian goals in war. For example Dr. Appia, while observing the Schleswig-Holstein war in 1864, came to believe that civilian efforts to assist those wounded should be based in part on religious devotion. Thus he saw those civilian volunteers as an army of Christians implementing their faith. Others associated with the Red Cross movement would also see in Christian good works the motivation for activities and adherences to the Geneva Convention of 1864. Yet Moynier, so influential in the ICRC's early years, declared that the agency was not a faith-based organization.

Religion aside, the result of the convergence of national self-interest and humanitarian spirit in 1864 was the first Geneva Convention for Victims of War, which was signed by 12 Western states including Prussia and France (the United States gave its consent to be bound in 1882, after much lobbying by Clara Barton, the founder of the American Red Cross and a strong supporter of the ICRC). Its primary contribution was to neutralize the war-wounded and the medical personnel who tended them. After these legal developments occurred there were many opportunities to test Dunant's vision in practice. (However, after 1867 Dunant was no longer able to play a large role in the organization he envisioned. Financial scandals and debt associated with his business dealings, as well as a strained, competitive relationship with Moynier, led to Dunant's resignation from the organization in Geneva).

Development of the organization

Between 1870 and World War I, the ICRC would play a limited role in a number of wars. In addition, its central position as leader of Red Cross humanitarian protection came under attack from various circles. The French wanted to move the headquarters of the RC Movement to

Paris, where the French aid society would have played the leading role. Slightly later the Russians sought an expanded role within the RC Movement, with the Russian czar seeing himself as a major humanitarian figure. In general, these four decades witnessed humanitarian principles being transformed by nationalism and patriotism, leaving in their wake Dunant's original dreams of universal and neutral protection. By and large, the ICRC offered money to national Red Cross societies and encouraged others to report on activities undertaken. It did not, however, attempt to provide assistance to the wounded as a strong, independent actor on the ground.

Box 1.1   Resolutions adopted 26–29 October 1863, Preparatory Conference

Art. 1   Each country shall have a Committee whose duty it shall be, in time of war and if the need arises, to assist the Army Medical Services by every means in its power. The Committee shall organize itself in the manner which seems to it most useful and appropriate.

Art. 2   An unlimited number of Sections may be formed to assist the Committee, which shall be the central directing body.

Art. 3   Each Committee shall get in touch with the Government of its country, so that its services may be accepted should the occasion arise.

Art. 4   In peacetime, the Committees and Sections shall take steps to ensure their real usefulness in time of war, especially by preparing material relief of all sorts and by seeking to train and instruct voluntary medical personnel.

Art. 5   In time of war, the Committees of belligerent nations shall supply relief to their respective armies as far as their means permit: in particular, they shall organize voluntary personnel and place them on an active footing and, in agreement with the military authorities, shall have premises made available for the care of the wounded.

They may call for assistance upon the Committees of neutral countries.

Art. 6   On the request or with the consent of the military authorities, Committees may send voluntary medical personnel to the battlefield where they shall be placed under military command.

Art. 7   Voluntary medical personnel attached to armies shall be supplied by the respective Committees with everything necessary for their upkeep.

Art. 8   They shall wear in all countries, as a uniform distinctive sign, a white armlet with a red cross.

Art. 9 The Committees and Sections of different countries may meet in international assemblies to communicate the results of their experience and to agree on measures to be taken in the interests of the work.

Art. 10 The exchange of communications between the Committees of the various countries shall be made for the time being through the intermediary of the Geneva Committee.

Independently of the above Resolutions, the Conference makes the following Recommendations:

a   that Governments should extend their patronage to Relief Committees which may be formed, and facilitate as far as possible the accomplishment of their task.

b   that in time of war the belligerent nations should proclaim the neutrality of ambulances and military hospitals, and that neutrality should likewise be recognized, fully and absolutely, in respect of official medical personnel, voluntary medical personnel, inhabitants of the country who go to the relief of the wounded, and the wounded themselves;

c   that a uniform distinctive sign be recognized for the Medical Corps of all armies, or at least for all persons of the same army belonging to this Service; and, that a uniform flag also be adopted in all countries for ambulances and hospitals.

(www.icrc.org)

Hence Moynier and others at the ICRC sought to promote the development of national RC societies in the Western world. They did not desire to develop a strong centralized organization in Geneva which dictated activities to those aid societies. Had they tried to develop a strong centralized authority, their efforts probably would have been rejected, as national RC societies were moving closer to their country's military. In many respects this is not difficult to understand. Military commanders did not want charitable do-gooders to get in the way during armed conflict. Yet they could also see the benefit of receiving additional money and support for their soldiers. Thus instead of allowing independent Red Cross societies to develop within the nation, political leaders sought to nationalize and militarize the role of the national RC societies as much as possible. This has resulted in limited autonomy for RC societies in relation to national civilian and military authorities, but considerable autonomy for the RC societies *vis-à-vis* the ICRC.

One could see the militarization of the Red Cross societies in the Franco–Prussian War (1870–1871). The Prussians subsumed the national aid societies into an arm of the military's medical branch. Prince Pless directed that voluntary aid assistance and nurses from the aid societies be placed under the command of the army's medical staff.[7] The Prussian initiatives were efficient and well received, so much so that other RC societies sought to replicate that militarization. (The French, on the other hand, were neither well prepared for the war nor well informed of their obligations under the Geneva Convention of 1864.)

An additional problem which the ICRC encountered during this time was the development of a neutral emblem to represent the Movement. The ICRC had opted for a red cross against a white background (the inverse of the Swiss flag). This was not a welcome symbol for many in the Islamic world due to the association of a cross with Christianity and the tortured history between the Christian West and the Islamic East during the Crusades. In the 1870s, the Ottoman (Turkish) aid society opted for a red crescent instead. Consequently, the ICRC decided to accept this symbol and thereby avoided a disagreement with the Ottoman Empire. Multiple symbols, however, which later grew to three when Iran adopted the Red Lion and Sun, symbolized the fragmentation of the Movement and the difficulty of getting unified, neutral action in the face of national and cultural differences. Once the 1929 diplomatic conference on the laws of war, comprised of states, accepted multiple emblems as neutral signs in armed conflict, however, the issue of multiple RC emblems was set in legal stone.

The first major challenges

World War I and the inter-war years

World War I was a significant event in the history of the ICRC. The ICRC expanded its original mandate, which had focused on wounded soldiers, to helping civilians and prisoners of war. It also spoke out against the use of certain weapons, such as poisonous gas. It took up the plight of refugees and the internally displaced. The war confirmed the need for ICRC field action, as it was better placed than national RC societies in the various belligerent nations to implement neutral policies.

Gustave Ador, president of the ICRC during the war, sent delegates (Swiss attorneys, doctors, professors) to various military camps to stop reprisals against POWs (prisoners of war) and improve their material conditions.[8] Conditions in POW camps varied considerably from region to region. Various brutalities were committed by the Russians against their German prisoners, including lack of food, exposure to harsh weather conditions, and forced hard labor. Additional complaints were leveled against the Germans' harsh medical treatments (e.g. lack of chloroform during surgery). Other POW camps (British, French, and Japanese) were run relatively humanely, providing food and reading materials for captured soldiers. More important for the reputation of the ICRC was the fact that in most cases conditions in camps improved after ICRC delegates visited.

Additional ICRC activities during World War I were equally important. The ICRC set up various offices/warehouses to assist in the tracing of healthy and wounded soldiers held by their enemies. To facilitate these activities numerous volunteers poured into the ICRC's offices in Geneva to collect letters and inquiries about soldiers. Inquiries were then sent to national governments to see if additional information could be obtained. By the end of the war, the agency had handled over two million letters concerning the status of soldiers.[9] In addition, parcels and packages were sent to the ICRC to distribute to soldiers in POW camps.

All in all, despite the inhumane events of World War I, including the use of poisonous gas, the ICRC emerged as a respected moral authority, driven by humanitarian principles. At various points during the war, the ICRC reminded the warring parties of their obligations under the Geneva Convention and criticized the barbarity of the war. In recognition of these endeavors it was awarded the 1917 Nobel Peace Prize. It can be mentioned, however, that the French-speaking ICRC, based in Geneva and with limited resources, had concentrated its actions on the western front. This was probably not so much evidence of intentional partiality as evidence of underdeveloped communications and logistics.

In between the two world wars, the ICRC experienced a number of changes. First, it started to focus more systematically on those individuals detained in conflicts other than war. In Hungary in 1919, the ICRC attempted to gain access to political prisoners. Just as in cases of war, the ICRC did not ask which side was the aggressor and which was the defender, so in domestic troubles and tensions the ICRC attempted to see how the prisoners were being treated and chose not to inquire why they were being detained.

Second, it also devoted more attention to refugees uprooted by political events. The revolution in Russia which led to the communist takeover of that country produced millions of refugees who fled their homes. These individuals also required assistance, though the ICRC realized shortly that it alone could not support all the refugees in

Europe. Third, it expanded and systematized its actions in internal wars, notably in Spain in the 1930s. Already, ICRC involvement in the Balkans in the 1870s was involvement in internal conflicts from the point of view of the Ottoman Empire. But the Spanish Civil War confirmed the ICRC's emerging focus on internal war, even if it was internationalized by the participation of outside parties.

Fourth, it expanded its activities into Africa and other places outside Europe. For example, whereas it had played no direct role in the Boer War between Britain and the Boers of southern Africa around the turn of the century, by the 1930s it was deeply involved in the war resulting from the Italian conquest of Abyssinia (Ethiopia), at least on the Ethiopian side.[10]

These activities were in some ways logical extensions of previously developed humanitarian principles and programs. For the ICRC, persons being detained, for example, deserve certain protections whether they are detained as a result of an international war, an internal war, or internal troubles and tensions. And if this is true in Europe, why not in Africa and elsewhere? If combatants merit humanitarian protection when out of the hostilities, why not humanitarian protection for civilians, who were never supposed to be targets of the fighting anyway? The logic of humanitarian concern led to a type of mission creep in ICRC programming.

World War II

The ICRC compiled a mixed record during World War II. Despite the limited amount of resources and small, yet devoted staff (three individuals in 1939) the ICRC achieved some successes during WWII.[11] During this war the ICRC made over 11,000 detention visits, including to some Allied prisoners of war held by the Nazis and vice versa; delivered 445,702 tons of relief; and registered and assisted over 30 million persons during the war.[12]

There were also various limitations and fruitless attempts on the part of the ICRC to address the plight of vulnerable individuals caught in the midst of this war. The ICRC did not produce a significant record when dealing with soldiers captured by the Japanese, and the marginal achievements pertaining to the Holocaust would haunt the organization for decades to come. Of course we should remember that in this war the ICRC was dealing with illiberal governments (e.g. Japan, Germany, the Soviet Union) and since the basic principles of humanitarian protection are grounded in liberal thought (the value of individuals, human dignity, equality, etc.), then we should expect, as was the case in the Soviet Union and Japan, that illiberal governments would be less inclined to respect humanitarian principles.[13] Still, we should recall that the Nazis, who had a curious affection for legal rules and who were parties to the 1929 Geneva Convention for the Protection of Prisoners of War, provided more or less humane conditions for many Allied POWs. They were so obligated under that treaty. The situation was entirely otherwise for both Soviet POWs held by the Nazis and vice versa, as the Soviets had never accepted that treaty, and thus Berlin had no legal obligations under it *vis-à-vis* the USSR. It is difficult to discern which of these two states treated POWs held by them less humanely. This history suggests that the Geneva Conventions can at times have some humanitarian impact, even on illiberal states like Nazi Germany. It was also the case that the Nazis regarded especially Anglo-Americans as of Aryan stock and thus of acceptable race, which was not true of Nazi views of Slavic peoples. The ICRC was able to accomplish much relief work in some places, such as Greece, with the help of liberal countries such as Great Britain and Sweden. The Swedish Red Cross, with the help of the British navy, assisted civilians by delivering humanitarian supplies.[14] This was feasible due to the fact that both the Swedes and the British supported humanitarian endeavors in ways which illiberal states, such as the Japanese, did not. It was also the case that the British had political reasons for allowing the humanitarian work to go forward, being interested in good relations with Washington, where a pro-Greek lobby was influential.

While some in leadership positions at the ICRC were less than fully dynamic in protecting the welfare of Jews and others in concentration camps, it is worth noting that some individuals working for the ICRC in various countries were dynamic and creative in the ways that they found to protect the vulnerable. Thousands of volunteers were organized for humanitarian purposes by the ICRC. Furthermore, some ICRC delegates arranged for Jews to register for migration to Palestine, thus allowing them to escape the wrath of the Nazis.[15] Eventually, toward the end of the war, the ICRC was able to gain access to the Nazi concentration camps, but the delegates were forced to remain there until the Allied liberation of the camps.[16]

Despite its failure to protect German Jews and other German individuals regarded as sub-human by the Nazis (homosexuals, for example), the ICRC compiled an impressive record in its work with prisoners of war and aid to many civilians caught in the harsh realities of war. For these activities it was awarded the Nobel Peace Prize in 1944.

Box 1.2 Case study: the Holocaust

Unfortunately, World War II was not a complete success for the ICRC. The failure of the Western world to respond appropriately, first to German persecution and ethnic cleansing of the Jews, and then to their genocide, remains a blemish for many governments. This is also true of the ICRC. From 1933, the ICRC attempted to gain access to the concentration camps run by the Nazis throughout Europe. To do so, the ICRC first contacted the German Red Cross. This was ill-advised given that the German RC was being incorporated into the Nazi totalitarian state. The head of the German Red Cross, Ernst Grawitz, took part in the pseudo-medical experiments on the Jews during the Holocaust. Thus, when the ICRC sought assistance from the German RC, it was similar to asking Al Capone to look into illegal alcohol distribution during Prohibition. While the ICRC was able to negotiate some concentration camp visits prior to 1936, on the basis of permission granted by Berlin, it was unable to do so in a systematic and serious way.[17] The same was true in Austria before that state was merged with Germany in 1938. The ICRC did send some relief packages through the mail to prisoners in the Nazi concentration camps, but this was ended when there were reports that the relief was not always going to the prisoners. The then existing Geneva Conventions did not cover the treatment of civilians by their own government, or foreign civilians held by a belligerent. Moreover, international human rights law was not developed to any great extent until after World War II. Thus, while Berlin was legally obligated to treat Allied POWs humanely, it was not so legally restricted under treaty law when dealing with German detainees, or foreign civilians of Polish and similar origins. With regard particularly to German Jewish detainees, the ICRC had to seek access to them without appeal to international law.

Historians and other scholars have documented the failure of the ICRC to adequately respond to the Holocaust. The ICRC had learned of aspects of the genocide and debated a public plea for all the belligerents to adhere to humanitarian principles. At issue was a general appeal to protect various victims from the horrors of the war.[18] During a meeting on 12 October 1942, the ICRC Assembly (the governing body) decided against a public appeal concerning the Holocaust and other subjects.[19] So, when faced with some knowledge of genocide in Germany, which had reached the ICRC via private channels, the ICRC did not speak out, even in a careful way.

One may wonder whether an ICRC public statement would have made any difference after the Wannsee Conference in early 1942, when the Nazi leadership decided to move systematically from persecution, confinement, and deportation of the German Jews, with some acts of genocide, to their physical elimination on a major scale. From that time it was clear that the Nazis intended to kill as many Jews as possible, and they continued their efforts until the end of the war. Thus, it is doubtful that an ICRC statement could have stopped the Holocaust, given the ICRC's lack of public stature at the time. The silence of the Vatican was a different matter, given how prominent the Catholic Church was in the Western world, not to mention the fact of many politically active German Catholics.

Apart from the issue of the public statement, the more damaging question is why we do not find more dynamic quiet diplomacy on the part of the ICRC when dealing with the Holocaust, especially once it knew it was facing some kind of genocide in the death camps. ICRC leaders like President Max Huber and his alter ego C. J. Burckhardt, both Swiss Germans, did not vigorously press the Nazi leadership on the question of the camps, even quietly.[20] The best answer to this question probably lies in Swiss neutrality on the part of the government in Bern, a neutrality that historically contributed to ICRC achievements but which in this case impeded them. Many Swiss leaders, both in Bern and Geneva, while not openly anti-Semitic, were concerned about not offending or provoking the Germans. There was also the fact that Burckhardt, who was close to many German leaders, was trying to mediate the conflict with the British and German authorities. Hence he did not always prioritize strictly humanitarian efforts in favor of the Jews. The primary reason for the rejection of any public statement was the fear of compromising the Swiss government's position of neutrality, which translated into a policy of appeasement in order to safeguard the independence of the country. After all, the Nazis did have contingency plans for the invasion of Switzerland. This willingness in Bern to accommodate certain Nazi interests was true not only for humanitarian issues but also for the banking industry as well.[21] So the Swiss government turned back a number of German Jewish refugees. And Swiss banks, with the approval of their government, helped the Nazis convert gold and other resources, some of them stolen, into convertible currency.

An assertive ICRC, as a Swiss-dominated organization, could have provoked the wrath of the Nazis and this in turn could have had negative consequences for the Swiss state. So individuals such as Philippe Etter, who was a member of the ICRC Assembly as well as the president of the Swiss Federal Council, persuaded the other members of the Assembly to reject a public statement. To this day, some ICRC officials believe they could not have made public comment on the Holocaust without jeopardizing the organization's ongoing work with POWs on both sides of the Allied–German conflict.

Whether a public statement would have affected Nazi policy is, from one view, beside the point. A close reading of the historical record suggests that the ICRC chose to defer to Swiss national interests instead of adopting dynamic quiet diplomacy to maximize its efforts in defense of the victims of the death camps. One major value that was at stake was the reputation of the ICRC for vigorous and well considered efforts devoid of favoritism to particular states. The ICRC's policy positions concerning the Holocaust injured the reputation of the organization, at least to some extent.

chose to defer to swiss interests

The Cold War

The development of the Cold War presented new challenges for the ICRC. After World War II, the organization found itself short of funds. During the war the belligerents themselves had provided some funds for the transport of relief and other ICRC roles. This funding ceased with the end of the war. So the ICRC engaged in radical "downsizing" in the late 1940s. Also, the Swedish Red Cross led a move to internationalize the ICRC's Assembly. While this move ultimately failed, it indicated for a time some considerable dissatisfaction with the organization even in the liberal West.[22] At the time of the First Arab–Israeli war in 1948, there was a real question whether the ICRC would survive. The organization sought to use that conflict not only to help victims of war, but also to prove to the world that it was still a viable institution.

In an important success, the ICRC was able to further international humanitarian law (IHL) by contributing to the negotiation of the 1949 Geneva Conventions. The ICRC served as the secretariat for the Red Cross and governmental meetings leading up to the diplomatic conference called by the Swiss government. The latter is the depositary state for IHL, which means that it receives notices of state consent and reservations, and thus keeps the official record of who is bound by what IHL provision. The four 1949 Geneva Conventions remain the central edifice in contemporary IHL, a legal firewall against barbarism even in war.

Yet the ICRC encountered many new difficulties. Its funding remained precarious. Its staff remained small and amateurish. Its top policy-making body, the Assembly, left much to be desired in strategic thinking and effective oversight. Despite these problems, the ICRC found itself as never before with a global role involving extensive operations in Asia, Africa, and the Western Hemisphere—in addition to its historical focus on Europe. It continued to try to protect victims of conflicts not only in war but also during domestic unrest.

The fact that the ICRC encountered resistance from numerous communist countries in upholding the values of the Geneva Conventions was certainly among the major obstacles it faced. Most communist countries including the Soviet Union, China, North Korea, and North Vietnam, viewed the ICRC as an appendage of Western, capitalist governments such as the United States or Switzerland. The communist governments mostly chose to ignore requests by the ICRC for access to prisoners, whether they were soldiers or civilians.

It is also true that some Western states, such as the French in Algeria or the Americans in Vietnam, did not always cooperate fully with the ICRC. But Western states were the primary donors to the ICRC during the Cold War, and in abstract, theoretical, or philosophical terms, there was no fundamental conflict between Western democratic values, based on individual civil and political rights, and RC humanitarian values based on impartial concern for the individual in need. Hence, Western democratic states have always been the primary financial donors to the ICRC.

Thus, at various points during the Cold War, we see the ICRC, despite its best efforts, impotent to assist vulnerable individuals when states blocked their access. Yet at the end of the Cold War, in a way similar to the end of the World War I, despite the frustrations and setbacks, the ICRC finally emerged from this historical period with its reputation intact and its position in international relations solidified. In the following section we will discuss some of the challenges that the ICRC faced during the Cold War and the ways in which these events transformed the organization.

Expanding international humanitarian law

During the Cold War, the ICRC was successful in the further development of international humanitarian law. In 1949 the ICRC had played a central role, as noted, in the codification of the four Geneva Conventions for victims of war including civil wars. These built on and expanded previous conventions and were, to a considerable extent, based on the activities of the ICRC during World War II. Later, in 1977, in a development that did not originate with the ICRC, two additional protocols were added to the 1949 Geneva Conventions. Protocol I expanded the coverage of IHL in international war.[23] Protocol II considerably developed IHL for high-threshold internal wars, significantly adding to Common Article 3 from 1949, which at that time was the only piece of IHL treaty law establishing minimal standards for humanitarian protection in civil wars. While the ICRC in the mid-1970s did not play the central role in drafting that it had played in the run-up to the 1949 Geneva Conventions, nevertheless the ICRC did make a number of contributions to the evolution of the 1977 Protocols. Unfortunately, the application of IHL was often sorely lacking in various conflicts, including Korea, Algeria, Vietnam, and the Middle East.

Communist countries

As noted earlier, the ICRC has historically had difficult relations with many illiberal governments. This was especially evident during the Cold War. Communist countries such as China, the Soviet Union, North Korea, and North Vietnam did not often given serious attention to IHL. The Geneva Conventions and the humanitarian principles on which the ICRC based its work were not consistent with the ideology of many communist countries. Humanitarianism, and the liberal philosophy on which it is based, stresses respect for the individual and protection of human dignity. These were not the central values of communist states. While communist countries professed to be committed to the eventual liberation and emancipation of the human being, in fact most communist regimes were based on considerable political and other forms of repression. After all, communist theorists advocated a dictatorship in order to advance their cause. Furthermore, they stressed the importance of inevitable material forces rather than individual integrity, autonomy, and freedom. Cooperation between communist countries and the ICRC was almost certainly further hindered by the belief that the ICRC was a pawn of the West.

The practical impact of these philosophical differences was a general lack of ICRC access to POWs and political prisoners held by communist powers. During the Korean War (1950–1953) the ICRC sought repeatedly and unsuccessfully to conduct detention visits for individuals held by North Korea. This same pattern was repeated during the Vietnam War, as the ICRC failed to obtain access to American flyers shot down and held by the North Vietnamese. The North Vietnamese did not respect the Geneva Conventions, tortured enemy prisoners captured during the war, and, by and large, refused to deal with ICRC delegates. It is also true that there were many violations of IHL by the

United States and its principal ally in the south, the government of the Republic of Vietnam. Communist violations, however, in relative terms, were more systematic.

There were a few instances in which a communist country cooperated with the ICRC. In the 1979 border war between China and North Vietnam, both sides agreed to detention visits by ICRC delegates. That both countries were communist apparently provided the space for allowing neutral humanitarian protection. An additional example of communist cooperation arose in Eastern Europe. During martial law in Poland in the early 1980s, the Polish government granted the ICRC access to political prisoners. This was one of the rare instances in which the ICRC was able to work inside an Eastern European communist regime. It is worth remembering that the Soviet Union was in decline in the 1980s and the Polish government needed all the sources of legitimacy that it could muster. We see a limited window of opportunity opening for the ICRC based on the broader political environment.

Another example of cooperation between the ICRC and a communist government can be found in Cambodia in 1980. The invasion of the country by (North) Vietnam left that communist government with responsibility for lands that had been made destitute in every way by the radical agrarian communists known as the Khmer Rouge. In that situation, Hanoi permitted its surrogate Hun Sen government in Phnom Pen to allow a major relief operation for several years managed by the ICRC, in tandem with UNICEF. By this time in Southeast Asia, the pro-Western Republic of Vietnam had ceased to exist, and the United States had withdrawn most of its military presence in the immediate region.

Cambodia in 1980 was reminiscent of Hungary in 1956. In the latter case, the Soviet invasion of its communist neighbor and ally, which was flirting with more liberal forms of government, left the communist giant with responsibility for feeding a disrupted Hungarian nation on the eve of a harsh winter. Hence, Moscow allowed the ICRC (and other actors like the UNHCR) to provide humanitarian relief for a time. The ICRC won high marks for its organizational skills in this operation, but its efforts to visit political prisoners were stymied by the usual lack of permission from most communist countries most of the time during the Cold War.

The Cuban Missile Crisis of 1962 showed, however, a certain Soviet respect for the ICRC. To make a complicated story brief, one can say that Moscow, looking for a way to retreat from an exceedingly dangerous policy of installing attack missiles in Cuba, accepted a role for the ICRC. The question arose as to who might verify that Soviet shipping in and out of Cuba was peaceful, not a violation of the US quarantine/blockade, and in keeping with efforts to defuse the crisis and avoid nuclear war by removing the missiles. The ICRC and the principal states involved, plus the UN, all agreed that the ICRC should appoint a group of Swiss citizens to perform the inspections. The ICRC, after internal debate, agreed to act beyond its normal mandate in the interests of peace, as long as its personnel did not have to pass public judgment about Soviet foreign and security policies. In the final analysis, the crisis was resolved without the projected inspection team being formed. Nevertheless, the diplomatic agreement that had been quietly reached indicated the ICRC was acceptable to the Soviets in the most serious crisis of the Cold War.[24]

Decolonization and national liberation

Starting in about 1955 and accelerating during the 1960s and 1970s, the decolonization process was coterminous with many national liberation movements in Africa and Asia. The process was usually politically bumpy and often violent. For the ICRC this meant a number of operations outside of Europe where the organization was not very well known, where it did not always have a strong national RC society to work with, where logistical obstacles to effective programs were enormous, and where white ICRC personnel from a European state were not always initially well received.

The Nigerian Civil War, covered in some detail in a later chapter, presented a good picture of many of the problems faced by the ICRC, and consequently overcome by it (at least in a relative sense) over a considerable period of time.

In fact, during any given year during the Cold War, the ICRC might be found devoting a substantial part of its budget to relief operations in places like Nigeria, or Ethiopia and neighboring states, or Rhodesia/Zimbabwe, or Angola, or Mozambique, or Cambodia. Visits to various categories of prisoners, while usually less expensive than relief operations, were nevertheless often of long-running duration, as in the Republic of South Africa where Nelson Mandela and many others were visited over a number of years. To give yet another example, both relief and prisoner visits went on for considerable time in Sri Lanka.

Challenges in the Western Hemisphere

Most states in the Western Hemisphere, excepting in the Caribbean, had obtained legal independence much earlier, so the situation was generally different from Africa and Asia. Also, the Cold War affected the region mostly indirectly even if in powerful ways. That is, the main battle lines of the Cold War were often elsewhere, as in Central Europe (Germany and Eastern Europe), or East Asia (Korea) or Southeast Asia (Vietnam), with the exception of the Cuban Missile Crisis (1962). Still, part of the reason for exceptional detention in the South American southern cone in the 1970s and 1980s was because of the perception by conservative factions that "left-wing subversives" threatened the nation. Violence in Central America in the 1980s, particularly in El Salvador, Nicaragua, and Grenada, was tied to the broader Cold War, with "leftist" and "rightist" factions battling for political control in very nasty ways, with important foreign support on both sides for much of the time.

In the 1970s and 1980s the ICRC was faced with authoritarian and military regimes in much of South America. In places such as Argentina, Brazil, Columbia, El Salvador, Chile, and Guatemala, the ICRC attempted to gain access to those individuals detained for political reasons. In some states, the military and political leaders refused to give ICRC delegates immediate access to detainees. This was true, for example, in Argentina under military rule in early 1977. Months later the ICRC was able to have contact with detainees, although there were continued threats against those detainees who spoke about the conditions in which they were kept. At other times there were hide-and-seek tactics: hiding, moving, or limiting access to certain security detainees and thus hindering the humanitarian activities of the ICRC. It was during this period that these South American "national security states" began the widespread practice of the "forced disappearance" of persons.[25] These policies of forced disappearance and torture, sometimes opposed by US governments like the Carter administration, were later adopted by the George W. Bush administration after 11 September 2001.

ICRC delegates in a country such as Chile or Argentina compiled lists of individuals who were missing. These lists were then presented to the authorities. The response given by these governments was that these individuals were not under arrest and that the authorities had no knowledge of the whereabouts of the person in question. The ICRC was unable to locate many of these individuals, and merely able to document the fact that these individuals were missing. Countless numbers of the "disappeared" were killed. This is not to suggest that the ICRC was completely unsuccessful in its efforts in South America. Delegates made thousands of visits to detainees and helped secure the release of numerous individuals. Thus, while the ICRC was not able to provide humanitarian protection to all individuals who were vulnerable to the authorities, the organization continued to acquire a reputation for diligence and humanitarian commitment with regard to political prisoners, as with regard to its other activities.

These matters were to reappear after the Cold War during the era of terrorism and counter-terrorism, but this time it was the United States and its allies that were accused of forced disappearance and ghost detainees (see Chapter 6).

Organizational changes

At various points during the Cold War, events forced the ICRC to make changes in organizational structure and operations. These changes usually occurred slowly, over considerable time. The Nigerian Civil War (1967–1970) demonstrated to the world (via media coverage) and even to the ICRC itself, that a number of its policies and procedures needed rethinking. The ICRC entered this war without a well-developed strategy and was unable to cope with new challenges, such as intense media coverage, other humanitarian actors working in the country, lack of well-trained professional staff, and the political implications of some of its decisions. Following its controversial performance in the Nigerian Civil War, the ICRC agreed, without enthusiasm, to a review of Red Cross activities by a team of international scholars and officials. The result was the 1975 Tansley Report, which concluded that the Movement was indeed badly fragmented, with many weak national units, and that changes should be made to encourage more cooperation and common focus among the ICRC, the Federation, and the national RC societies. By implication, this report criticized the quality of ICRC leadership on these issues, which, as the "guardian of IHL" and founding agent of the Movement, had allowed the then-current situation to develop. In addition, the Tansley Report criticized the excessive secrecy in which the ICRC operated. This report eventually contributed marginally to gradual changes in how the ICRC conducted its affairs. (The Nigerian Civil War and the Tansley Report are further discussed in Chapter 4.)

Throughout the history of the ICRC, it has seen a number of initiatives which threatened its position in the Movement. In 1867 a world exposition was held in Paris. Some members of France's aristocracy and the French National Aid Committee wanted Paris, not Geneva, to take the lead in promoting humanitarianism.[26] Another threat emerged from Russia in 1883 at an International Red Cross conference. A Russian proposal was put forth to enlarge the role of the ICRC and the activities which it undertook. Most damaging of all was a proposal to enlarge and internationalize the all-Swiss Assembly, which is the top policy-making body of the organization.[27]

Later, after World War I, an American, Henry Davison, would propose and then create a League of Red Cross Societies that would challenge the authority of the ICRC. Davison, a behind-the-scenes leader of the American Red Cross, with close ties to President Wilson, sought to develop a strong, assertive RC Movement, led by the League, which in turn would be supported by the American Red Cross. The League of National RC Societies (later renamed the Federation) would deal with various problems, but especially health issues in peacetime. The ICRC, of course, recognized this attempt to supplant its authority. Although the ICRC could not prevent Davison's creation from coming to fruition, it tried to marginalize it as much as possible. In the end, the ICRC protected its place in providing humanitarian protection and assistance in situations of conflict, while the League was left to deal with natural disasters and other concerns in peacetime. Although the ICRC retained its pre-eminent position, it nevertheless had to acknowledge the existence of another body, the Federation, and relations between the two were far from harmonious for a long time.

The ICRC would also see an attempt to challenge its place in humanitarian protection from Count Bernadotte, the president of the Swedish Red Cross after World War II. In each instance, ICRC leaders carefully and skillfully saw these proposals defeated, or at the very least diluted, and their place at the center of the RC network reaffirmed (either through conferences or by self-declaration). Thus, it was not only national governments who sought to further their self-interest but also the constituent parts of the RC Movement. The end result was that the ICRC continued to operate more or less independently of both the Federation and of national RC societies, and of the International RC Conference which remained primarily a non-authoritative debating meeting.

From one view this situation presented beneficial features, in that the mono-national ICRC (at least via its Assembly) could operate—at least in principle—on the basis of an independent neutrality that the Federation and national RC societies could not always match. From another view, the independence of the ICRC often contributed to a fragmented Movement that failed to achieve its maximum potential in the domain of humanitarian affairs.

It is worth mentioning one last, ongoing external threat to the centrality of the ICRC's humanitarianism. During the Cold War, partly on the basis of technological changes such as ease of transnational communication and organization, one saw the rise of numerous non-governmental organizations (NGOs) such as Amnesty International, Human Rights

Watch, Doctors Without Borders, and World Vision. All of these NGOs took an interest in armed conflict and what the UN sometimes called "complex emergencies," and many of them ran relief programs in the field. In addition, from about 1970, international governmental organizations (IGOs) such as UNICEF and UNHCR and the World Food Programme (WFP) became more active regarding humanitarian relief in conflicts. These organizations now work in conflict zones which used to be reserved for the ICRC. The ICRC is no longer the only actor in the field, nor in some cases, the biggest actor on the scene. In the final chapter we will discuss whether the ICRC is still a relevant organization in light of these developments.

Conclusions

The origins of the ICRC can be found in Switzerland in the mid-nineteenth century. Originating with Dunant's humanitarian concerns from the Battle of Solferino and continuing through the works of Moynier, Maunoir, Appia, and Dufour, the ICRC evolved from a small private organization in Geneva to an agency treated as if it were an international organization, with a $1.4 billion budget, a staff of some 16,000, and humanitarian operations in all regions of the world. The ICRC continues to present itself as the guardian of international humanitarian law and founding agent of the RC Movement. It has extended its concern from sick and wounded combatants, to captured combatants, to civilians caught in wars and similar violence, to political prisoners. Although the Geneva Conventions were not always respected (or known) by soldiers (and probably quite a few policy-makers), over time ICRC activities sometimes had a definite impact on international relations.

The evolution of the organization was often slow and cautious. This was due to a number of factors, including the influence of Swiss political culture, such as discretion and reluctance to go public with criticism, its relationship with the national RC societies, as well as the realities of international relations and power politics. Some of these confines resulted in the controversial policies during World War II and especially the Holocaust.

Yet throughout its history the ICRC met criticism with changes. Gradually the organization (both delegates and administrators) became more professional. Over time the ICRC became increasingly efficient (delivering relief parcels, visiting POWs, etc.) and more active (sending out numerous delegates to all regions of the world). As the twentieth century progressed, the ICRC found creative ways to try to protect the dignity of those who were among the most vulnerable, maintaining a commitment, at least most of the time, to neutrality and a non-judgmental stance when confronted with the horrors of war.

Notes

1 Dunant, quoted in Patrick Turnbull, *Solferino: The Birth of a Nation* (New York: St. Martin's Press, 1985), 175.
2 Turnbull, *Solferino: The Birth of a Nation*, 157–59.
3 Caroline Moorehead, *Dunant's Dream: War, Switzerland and the History of the Red Cross* (New York: HarperCollins, 1999), 8. Henry Dunant, *A Memory of Solferino* (Geneva, Switzerland: ICRC, 1986), 126.
4 Jean-Jacques Rousseau, *The Social Contract* (London: Penguin, 1968), 56–57.
5 Moorehead, *Dunant's Dream*, 17. This committee became the ICRC. "Red Cross" was officially added in 1875.
6 John Hutchinson, *Champions of Charity: War and the Rise of the Red Cross* (Boulder, Colo.: Westview, 1996), 27.
7 Hutchinson, *Champions of Charity*, 119–21.
8 ICRC discretion about POW visits is not mandated by the GCs but rather was a practice eventually developed by the organization. This is a practice that continues to this day. This is ironic because Dunant believed in the value of publicity.
9 Moorehead, *Dunant's Dream*, 206.
10 An extremely important source for understanding not only this conflict but also the nature of the ICRC in historical perspective is Ranier Blaudendistel's *Between Bombs and Good Intentions: The International Committee of the Red Cross (ICRC) and the Italo-Ethiopian War, 1935–1936* (New York: Berghahn Books, 2005).
11 André Durand, *History of the International Committee of the Red Cross: From Sarajevo to Hiroshima* (Geneva, Switzerland: Henry Dunant Institute, 1984), 413.
12 ICRC, *Report of the International Committee of the Red Cross on its Activities during the Second World War* (Geneva, Switzerland: ICRC, 1948), 3 volumes and annexes.
13 Geoffrey Best, *Humanity in Warfare* (New York: Columbia University Press, 1980), 60.
14 Mark Mazower, *Inside Hitler's Greece: The Experience of Occupation, 1941–1944* (New Haven, Conn.: Yale University Press, 1993, 1995), especially pages 47, 337.
15 Durand, *From Sarajevo*, 438. See also André Durand, *The International Committee of the Red Cross* (Geneva, Switzerland: ICRC, 1981).
16 Drago Arsenijevic, *Otages volontaires des SS* (Paris: Editions France Empire, 1974, 1984).
17 See Francois Bugnion, *Le Comite international de la Croix-Rouge et la protection des victimes de la guerre* (Geneva, Switzerland: ICRC, 1994), 245.
18 ICRC Archives; Dossier CR 73; Carton 50, Fourth Draft, 16 September 1942, covering the subjects of: the effects of aerial bombardment on the civilian population; the effects of economic blockade on the civilian

population; the fate of those civilians of various nationalities who were detained, deported, or taken hostage; and treatment of prisoners of war.

19 This account is based on ICRC archives: procès-verbal of Assembly meetings, 1942–47, volume 18, organized by dates of meetings; supplemented by other archival sources such as staff PTT consultations with Assembly members regarding a public protest, found in G.85/127, CR73/8-/24. The role of the Assembly is discussed more fully in the next chapter.

20 Huber and Burckhardt basically allowed the ICRC to be supervised by Bern when the agency was dealing with matters that might be seen as sensitive in either Berlin or Bern. See Forsythe, *The Humanitarians*.

21 Adam Lebor, *Hitler's Secret Bankers: How Switzerland Profited from Nazi Genocide* (London: Simon and Schuster, 1997, 1999); see also Alan Cowell, "Switzerland's Wartime Blood Money," *Foreign Policy*, no. 107 (Summer 1997), 132–44.

22 Other forces were also at work, such as the desire of the Swedish Red Cross and its flamboyant leader, Count Bernadotte, to play a more central role in international humanitarian work. Bernadotte was assassinated in the Middle East while serving as a UN mediator on the question of Palestine.

23 In a subsequent chapter we pay further attention to these legal developments.

24 Francois Bugnion, "Confronting the Unthinkable," *Swiss Review of History*, 62/1, 62/2 (2012), 143–155 and 299–310.

25 It is interesting to observe that while the Argentine junta committed many atrocities against "domestic enemies" during 1976–1982, and did not cooperate fully with ICRC efforts to protect political prisoners, that same junta fought the war for the Falklands/Malvinas Islands more or less according to IHL. So while legal obligation and military honor and reciprocity, and possibly other factors, contributed to considerable respect for human dignity in armed conflict, no such humanitarian restraints were observed by the junta in its total war against domestic enemies.

26 Hutchinson, *Champions of Charity*, 79.

27 While the ICRC Assembly would remain all-Swiss, it did over time expand its membership. Although it began with only Protestant individuals from Geneva, it would by the 1920s invite other Swiss into the Assembly. Around this same time it opened its membership to Catholics and women. In the early 1990s it opened its professional staff to all nationalities.

2 Organization and management

In 1863 the International Committee of the Red Cross started with five volunteers and no budget. In 2015 the organization consisted of some 2,500 professional staff, another 11,500 support staff, and an annual budget of about $1.4 billion, as we noted already.[1] Over the years it relied less on volunteers and more on highly educated, trained professionals. Its budget, however, remained dependent on voluntary contributions rather than assessed dues, mostly from states and their international organizations like the European Union, and secondarily from RC societies. Obtaining information about how and why the ICRC made its decisions regarding particular problems is not easy, although the general process can be established. It was reasonably clear that the modern ICRC constituted a highly professional small bureaucracy that tried to combine creativity in the field with consistency of general policy, as established by its Geneva headquarters. Its determined commitment to help victims of political violence was noteworthy.

The Assembly and its Council

The governing board of the ICRC, its top policy-making organ when meeting in formal session, is called the Assembly. It has always been comprised only of Swiss citizens, numbering not more than 25. New members are selected by a vote of existing members. No outside party has any say about Assembly membership, not even the International RC

Conference or the RC Federation. From the standpoint of national law, the ICRC is a Swiss private association governed by its own statutes.

This arrangement is a historical accident, but there is a rationale for its continuation. Given permanent Swiss neutrality, which is not just a treaty provision (from 1815, reaffirmed in 1907) but a policy reality in contemporary international relations (the Swiss do not join military alliances), when the ICRC deals with conflict situations, its Assembly will contain no member from a fighting party. So Assembly membership guarantees a certain degree of neutrality which enables the organization to present itself to fighting parties as a strictly humanitarian actor.[2]

For the first 60 years of the organization, Assembly members were drawn exclusively from the French-speaking, Protestant citizens of Geneva—mostly from the upper-middle class. After World War I, membership was extended to Swiss-Germans and Swiss-Italians, some of whom were Catholic. The first woman was elected at roughly the same time. At the time of writing there has been one Jewish member of the Assembly. No racial minorities have ever been elected, there being few prominent non-white citizens of Switzerland. There have been a few union leaders and others said to be politically left of center in the Assembly, but most members have been drawn from politically conservative circles—lawyers, bankers, soldiers, medical doctors, and government officials.

The all-Swiss nature of the Assembly has been challenged from time to time, as already noted. In 2005 a Republican senator in Washington floated the idea that the Assembly's membership should be internationalized, with Americans holding about a third of the seats, since the United States provided about a third of the ICRC budget. But this idea did not get very far even within Republican circles in Washington, since such an arrangement would largely undermine the ICRC's image of neutrality in many conflicts.[3] How could the ICRC play any role as a neutral actor in conflicts involving the United States or NATO if Americans (and other individuals from NATO states) sat on the Assembly?

Before the 2005 tempest in a teapot in Washington over Assembly membership, the last major effort to change the Assembly's nature had been after World War II, when Count Bernadotte of the Swedish Red Cross talked of internationalizing the Assembly. But, particularly given the start of the Cold War, even he changed his mind and endorsed the status quo on this point. For one familiar with how the United Nations Security Council became mostly paralyzed because of deep divisions within its membership during the Cold War, the lack of political or strategic divisions within the ICRC Assembly, and its image of neutrality, was not something to be changed without careful consideration.[4]

all-Swiss composition

The all-Swiss composition of the Assembly has served Red Cross humanitarianism reasonably well since the 1860s, with several exceptions. During the 1930s, many Assembly members were politically conservative, and more than one Assembly member looked favorably on Italian fascism as a counterweight to both Nazism and Soviet communism. One result was more concern for appeasing Mussolini than a vigorous protection of war victims in Ethiopia.[5] During World War II (1939–1945) the Assembly was subjected to pressures from Swiss authorities in Bern, the latter being concerned to protect Switzerland from German invasion or other encroachment on its independence (as noted in the previous chapter).[6] During the Cold War (1947–1989), the Assembly was affected by widespread sentiments of anti-communism and a fear of the Soviet Union, an orientation which was then prevalent in Bern and throughout Switzerland. By the Nigerian Civil War (1967–1970), it was clear that the all-Swiss Assembly did not always recruit members with the strategic vision and organizational expertise to operate effectively in international relations. There was also the question of whether the all-Swiss Assembly had provided appropriate leadership for the RC Movement.

The role of the Assembly has now clearly been reduced within the organization. This has occurred for two related contemporary reasons. First, many of its members remain amateur volunteers when it comes to humanitarian action, being law professors, bankers, and doctors, etc., rather than professional humanitarians. However distinguished they might have been in their first careers, humanitarian politics and humanitarian operations demand a certain expertise that they do not always possess. Also, in the past the Assembly did not perform so well when trying to micromanage ICRC policy in complicated situations (as in the Nigerian Civil War). As a result, now it meets only six times a year. Its general role is similar to the parliament in many democracies, responding to and fine-tuning initiatives from the executive, setting general policies, and keeping a special eye on the general budgetary situation.

The ICRC Assembly, with its reduced importance and new awareness of the dangers of attempting to play too large a role, is in fact better constituted in 2015 than was the Governing Board of the American Red Cross in the past. The latter Board was rather recently characterized by too large a membership (50), inattentive members (many rarely attended meetings), serious infighting (five members forced out the then president in the winter of 2005–2006, with no formal vote and no paper record, one of whom then became the new president), with resulting controversial performance in responding to natural disasters like Hurricane Katrina in 2005.[7]

There is an Executive Council of the ICRC Assembly, which is made up of three elected members from that body plus the president and the permanent vice president of the organization. The role of this body is to make decisions on certain questions of strategy when the Assembly is not in session. In principle, it meets twelve times a year. In general, its role has proven more important than foreseen when this system was created. More than its parent Assembly, the Council persistently reviews the decisions taken by the professional side of the house, especially pertaining to supplemental budgetary requests and expenditures. These reflect changing operations in the field. Depending on the assertiveness of the elected members, they can even sometimes influence the president and his policy preferences. Still, meeting only about once a month, the Executive Council is not the manager of day to day affairs. This role falls to the Director General and Director of Operations, who themselves meet often with the President.

Because it is now recognized that Swiss national interests affected ICRC decisions particularly in the 1930s and 1940s,[8] there has been an attempt to enhance the independence of the organization. There is a headquarters agreement between Bern and Geneva, stipulating that the organization is off-limits to Swiss officials. In effect, Bern treats the ICRC as if it were an international inter-governmental organization. Moreover, it is now specified in ICRC regulations that one cannot be a member of the Assembly and hold public position in Switzerland. These measures seek to guard against what happened earlier, when Swiss officials were also members of the Assembly and elevated Swiss interests of state over neutral and impartial humanitarianism.

The president

Henry Dunant was never president of the ICRC. The organization was built under the leadership of President Gustave Moynier. It was consolidated under Presidents Gustave Ador and Max Huber. The latter was the first ICRC president from German speaking Switzerland.

The Assembly in modern times usually looks to the Swiss Confederation for its president. In 2015 the president was Peter Maurer, a Swiss German who had been a diplomat and official in the Swiss foreign ministry. The president preceding him was Jacob Kellenberger, another Swiss German and formerly the highest civil servant in the Swiss foreign ministry. Before him, ICRC president Cornelio Sommaruga, a Swiss Italian, was in the bureau of the Swiss foreign ministry dealing with economic affairs. And before him, President Alexander Hay, a French Swiss, was an official in the Swiss central bank.

judgment? *Organization and management* 33

One theory holds that Assembly members look to the circle of Swiss governing officials for their president because they do not trust their own judgment about world affairs; they therefore opt for someone with a proven track record in governmental positions. Another theory holds that Assembly members are conservative and do not want to choose a professional humanitarian who might "rock the boat"; they therefore opt for someone cautious enough to have had a successful career as a state official in Bern. Still a third theory is that Assembly members prefer to bring in someone from outside who at the start does not know so much about humanitarian law and policy; such a situation makes it more difficult for the President to dominate the Assembly, at least at the start of his tenure. So the argument runs, a professional humanitarian from inside the house would know far more about policy questions than the volunteer Assembly members. For whatever reason, in recent years the Assembly passed over two insiders who presented themselves as candidates to be president: Jacques Moreillon in 1986 and Pierre Kraehenbuehl in 2011. Both had been director-general, as well as holding other important ICRC positions.

It is a fact that when the ICRC president comes in from Swiss governing circles, he almost always knows little about the details of international humanitarian law, Red Cross principles, or the organization itself. One recent president asked the staff to explain the difference between neutrality and impartiality. Two recent presidents had to take a crash course, partially self-taught, on the 1949 Geneva Conventions and Additional Protocols. One recent president, despite being Swiss and having a career in foreign affairs, admitted that he knew virtually nothing about the ICRC when he took the job.[9] Yet the process has worked tolerably well in an overall sense. Presidents Hay, Sommaruga, and Kellenberger are all generally regarded as capable presidents who presided over changes in the organizations with considerable ability. Sommaruga was much more outgoing than Kellenberger, which is one example of the many ways these leaders differed, but there has not been a fundamental problem at the presidential level since the time of Marcel Naville (banker) and Eric Martin (medical doctor).[10]

President Kellenberger was the personification of the Swiss preference for quiet diplomacy compared to public argumentation. He was adept at tenacious maneuvering when he negotiated the Swiss relationship to the European Union in his previous position in Bern, and he showed the same traits at the ICRC. He kept the confidence of the Assembly, while positioning his allies in the key positions of director-general and director of operations. These three persons, who were in apparent agreement in previous years, control around 90 percent of the policy positions of the organization on questions of daily strategy and tactics. Only rarely did Kellenberger apparently shift preferences because of views in the Executive Council, and almost never because of views in the Assembly.

Box 2.1 Presidents of the ICRC

Name	Tenure	Primary profession
1 Henri Dufour	1863–1864	Soldier
2 Gustave Moynier	1864–1910	Lawyer
3 Gustave Ador	1910–1928	Financier, journalist, and publisher, president of Swiss Confederation
4 Max Huber	1928–1944	Lawyer, judge
5 C. J. Burckhardt	1944–1948	Professor, diplomat
6 Paul Ruegger	1948–1955	Diplomat
7 Leopold Boissier	1955–1964	Diplomat, professor, civil servant
8 Samuel Gonard	1964–1969	Soldier
9 Marcel Naville	1969–1973	Banker
10 Eric Martin	1973–1976	Doctor and professor of medicine
11 Alexandre Hay	1976–1986	Public official (central bank)
12 Cornelio Sommaruga	1987–1999	Public official (foreign ministry)
13 Jacob Kellenberger	2000–2011	Civil servant (foreign ministry)
14 Peter Maurer	2012–?	Diplomat, civil servant (foreign ministry)

Roger Gallopin, president of the Executive Council, was, in reality, the operational president of the ICRC during the official presidency of Eric Martin.

The exercise of influence at the top of the ICRC is not only opaque but also apparently contained within a collegial framework, with few formal votes taken. But no outsider knows very many details about contemporary policy making at the top, given that such information is restricted for forty years. We know now the details of ICRC policy

President

making in the exceptional matter of the Cuban missile crisis of 1962, but that is so only after several decades.

Contrary to some views, the ICRC President is more than just a public spokesman for policies decided by others. If he is so inclined, and this has been true of recent presidents, he not only appoints the top officials on the professional side of the house but also meets with them frequently to discuss operations in the field. So according to his preferences, he is involved in much nitty-gritty pertaining to daily operations and is not just primus inter pares in the Assembly.

Kellenberger did not cut a strong public figure in RC and diplomatic circles, certainly by comparison to Sommaruga. But much of the ICRC's work occurs through quiet diplomacy, where a certain personal warmth and attention to detail are assets. So Kellenberger, like Alexander Hay, is likely to be well regarded in historical perspective despite the lack of notoriety in the media. He faced some controversies about his management style. Like Sommaruga, Kellenberger did not hesitate to go into the minute details of questions that interested him. Unlike Sommaruga, Kellenberger did not try to micromanage everything, including allocation of scarce parking spaces at headquarters, but rather was more interested in some questions compared to others. He defended the organization vigorously when it was attacked by ultra-nationalist elements in Washington during controversies about US treatment of enemy detainees after 11 September 2001 (see Chapter 6). Yet he still retained the confidence of high Bush officials, perhaps because of his insistence on discretion and mostly absence of strong public comments. Whether retiring personalities like Kellenberger and Hay are well positioned to exercise leadership in the RC Movement is an interesting question. It is one thing to negotiate quietly with governments, while it is another thing to try to mobilize a fragmented movement without public and charismatic leadership. Kellenberger's objective was to emphasize quiet reliability and predictability.

The transition from Kellenberger to Peter Maurer was without major controversy. Maurer was more open and accessible than his predecessor, with a less reserved demeanor. Maurer without question was more adept at cocktail diplomacy. But major policy changes were hard to discern from changing personnel at the top. Recent presidents have tended to focus on relations with governments and their international organizations, which leaves the permanent vice president, in 2015 Christine Beerli, the space to exercise influence regarding relations with the RC Federation and the rest of the RC Movement. Maurer made a number of decisions about new personnel in the Directorate. But given the Swiss tradition of compromise and collegiality, any major disputes at the top were well concealed from outsiders. When it came to making ICRC policy, there was vigorous debate up and down the organization, but in the last analysis the house apparently functioned without major and debilitating internal squabbles. A strong commitment to its mandate seemed to permeate the organization in 2015.

The Directorate and professional staff

Since about 1970 there has been a power shift inside the ICRC. Increasingly, specific policy for this or that conflict is made not by the Assembly but by the president and the other full time humanitarians who make up the Directorate and professional staff.

The Directorate is basically the cabinet government of the ICRC, headed by the director-general who is, in effect, the ICRC's prime minister. ICRC policy-making is similar to French politics. France has the president, prime minister, and cabinet, while the ICRC has its president, director-general, and Directorate. In the Directorate are the officials in charge of communication and information technology, international law and policy, operations, financial resources and logistics, and human resources (personnel). These are the departments or divisions within the ICRC, providing leadership for the geographical and functional offices that do the grass roots work.[11]

In the recent past President Kellenberger worked well with director-general Angelo Gnaedinger (sometimes on leave for reasons of health) and Director of Operations Pierre Kraehenbuehl (sometimes director-general despite his relative youth). This group was where most key decisions were made, although they consulted with a variety of other persons such as the permanent vice president (for a long time Jacques Forster, the loyal long-time number two regardless of who was president), and numerous advisers in the office of the Directorate.

When Peter Maurer was selected as president in 2011, Pierre Kraenenbuehl had also put himself forward for the top spot as already noted. He had served as both director-general and director of operations. Having been passed over by the Assembly, he resigned and became head of the UN refugee organization for Palestinian refugees (UNRWA). Maurer then appointed Yves Daccord, former Director of Communications, to be director-general. Daccord had definite views about the operational side of the house, and his top-down style did not always sit well with the rest of the organization. Nevertheless Maurer reappointed him for a second term, and the two key officials found a way to cooperate despite some outside speculation about friction.

consult with professional side

  In ICRC policy making, there was a persistent effort to consult with those on the professional side of the organization who had direct knowledge of the facts in the field. In the history of the organization, there was an ethos of taking into account "the man on the ground." In modern times the man on the ground might in fact be a woman. Whereas up until the early 1990s the ICRC was 99 percent Swiss from top to bottom (with the exception of a few persons of French nationality in professional positions), from the early 1990s the ICRC staff was internationalized. This change was driven by the organization's need to recruit and retain persons with various specializations. After all, how many experts in tropical diseases are produced by Swiss medical schools? How many graduates of Swiss universities speak one of the languages of the Islamic world and know in detail the Koran? There was also a need for more general delegates, given the expanded ICRC operations around the world. By 2015 about half of the ICRC's professional staff of 2,500 were non-Swiss. Positions on the professional side, up through the director-generalship itself, were open to any staff person, regardless of nationality.

  At the time of writing, there were three females in the Directorate. Of its five members, one was German, one Australian, and one British. In the Assembly, there were four females plus the permanent vice president. Professional staff recruitment went well in Europe and North America, and many bilingual persons (French and English) were attracted to work for the ICRC. For a given year in contemporary times, the ICRC received about 20,000 applications for various positions. Only about 5 percent of professional staff, however, came from outside the north Atlantic area. (By contract, most of the ICRC's support staff, hired by field delegations and numbering over 10,000 each year, was non-Western.) The organization did have a problem, however, in retaining staff. The field work could be dangerous and exhausting. Many delegates worked on short-term contracts. Normal family life was difficult for ICRC staff, working as they did in the danger zones of the world. Consequently, turnover was high and retention of specialized staff was low. In recent years, of those starting out, about 75 percent of staff left after three years.

  As was mentioned before, the ICRC consists of some 11,500 field workers, over 10,000 of whom are native to the area in which they are working. While this fact is beneficial in the sense that cultural and linguistic consistencies tend to be more prevalent, unlike expatriates, local workers do not, in many cases, have the freedom to exit a situation if it proves to be dangerously hostile. In 2003, a clear example of this danger was illustrated by the targeting of Iraqi field workers in

Baghdad.[12] This is yet another reason why retention of staff can be difficult, especially in areas overwhelmed by war.

Despite all of this, the ICRC has been known for the sterling quality of its delegates in the field. These role models include perhaps Marcel Junod, during the era of the Spanish Civil War and World War II, Friedrich Born in Nazi-occupied Hungary, and André Rochat, in Yemen after World War II.[13] This tradition has been carried over into modern situations like the Balkan Wars of the 1990s and Somalia during the early 1990s, where ICRC personnel drew widespread praise for their diligence and pragmatic creativity in the face of grave dangers.

The delegate's role was not an easy one. In the midst of conflict, where amenities were unreliable, the delegate was to negotiate with fighting parties, organize and manage relief, obtain knowledge about hidden prisoners, trace missing persons, educate about IHL in locally meaningful ways, stay in touch with various RC and diplomatic circles, handle the press without violating rules for discretion, and submit a flood of reports to Geneva.

Since the end of the Cold War, numerous professional ICRC staff members have been killed in the line of duty, including the head of delegation in Bosnia in the 1990s. In 1996, six RC staff, working with the ICRC, were intentionally murdered in Chechnya. By comparison in the internationalized Syrian civil war from 2011, where ICRC expatriate staff had limited room to maneuver, over 40 staff members of the Syrian Arab Red Crescent, direct partners of the ICRC, were killed by one fighting party or another.

Finances

There is no assessed payment system to fund the activities of the ICRC. States can become parties to IHL treaties without becoming obligated to pay for the humanitarian protection of victims of war. For ICRC humanitarian activities, there is nothing comparable to the UN system of assessed dues, which are based primarily on a state's ability to pay. The RC Federation has a system of assessed dues from member RC societies, but the ICRC does not. One probable reason is that many sovereign states would object to required payments to a non-state party like the ICRC. Federation dues are assessed on putatively private RC societies, not states.

For much of its history the ICRC was in dire straits financially speaking. This was true after both world wars, when the organization downsized in major ways, driven by lack of contributions. In 1935, for example, the organization had a staff of 11, the majority of whom were typists to handle correspondence.[14] Tables 2.1–2.3 detail contributions to the ICRC.

For 2016 the ICRC asked for contributions amounting to about $1.6 billion. Slightly less than 85 percent of ICRC income was normally provided by voluntary state contributions. The United States was the leading donor, providing just under 30 percent of ICRC income in most years.

The other leading Western states, and the European Union, followed as major donors.

The ICRC operates on the basis of a core or headquarters budget, designed to cover essential costs, including headquarters support for field operations, and then a supplementary budget designed to cover needs in the field as they are anticipated. Unexpected emergencies result in supplemental appeals. While making its own financial calculations, the ICRC cooperates with the coordinated UN fundraising for all humanitarian/relief operations. UN fundraising

Table 2.1 2013 contributions to the ICRC (Swiss francs)

	Source	Contribution *(in Swiss francs)*
1	Governments	1,029,576,805
2	EU	88,238,355
3	IGOs	2,367,428
4	National RC societies	40,018,587
5	Other Public sources	7,503,838
6	Other Private sources	51,293234

All figures from ICRC Annual Reports.

Table 2.2 2013 contributions to the ICRC by governments, total, all forms, top five (Swiss francs)

	Country	Contribution *(in Swiss francs)*
1	US	260,074,721
2	UK	163,248,877
3	Switzerland	119,802,624
4	Sweden	69,831,180
5	Norway	63,936,304

Table 2.3 2013 contributions to the ICRC, total, all forms, national RC societies, top five (Swiss francs)

	Country	Contribution (in Swiss francs)
1	Norway	10,178,641
2	Sweden	4,224,559
3	Japan	3,952,821
4	UK	3,900,695
5	Canada	2,862,554

Most of the rest of ICRC operations were covered by voluntary donations from various national RC societies. Again, the Western ones were consistently the most generous. The Japanese RC, Western aligned, was the third most generous. Private donations rounded out the picture, including gifts in cash or kind not only from individuals but also from foundations, corporations, and even some non-governmental organizations.

In fact, while a typical ICRC total expenditure per year of about $1.4 billion was a sizable increase when compared with five years prior, this sum was small potatoes in relative terms compared to other public spending. In the United States, the two presidential candidates in 2012 spent over $2.6 billion in campaign advertising. US military spending in 2013 was over $618 billion when expenditures in Iraq and Afghanistan were added to the basic Department of Defense budget. States spent much more on war planning and war fighting than in coping with the victims of wars and other conflicts.

There were few controversies about ICRC expenditure of funds. There were multiple audits, both internal and external. The financial dealings of the organization were fully transparent and mind-numbing in detail. Given a Swiss tradition of great attention to detail, honesty, and propriety (some might say at least outside Swiss banking circles), there was almost never a charge of misappropriated funds.[15]

ICRC core administrative costs including for fund raising were slightly over 10%, a very good figure in relative terms. There was no doubt that by comparison with NGO relief actors, ICRC staff were well paid and well supported. The ICRC policy on this matter was that ICRC personnel should be well taken care of in order for them to do their job properly. Moreover, if one is going to retain well-trained and experienced personnel, one has to pay them at a rate, and with benefits, that will keep them from joining the UN or other organizations. In certain situations the ICRC decided not to use new vehicles and state-of-the-art communications systems in the field, because these things invited theft and danger to staff.

Conclusion

Over time, most organizations develop an organizational culture: a set of ideas about basic values and how to implement them.[16] For example, one scholar sees the UN refugee office (similar to the ICRC in that it does humanitarian protection and assistance) in these highly critical terms: the UNHCR is supposedly very conservative, resistant to change, inhospitable to the ideas of outsiders, with an arrogant leadership and some insensitivity to some of the beneficiaries of its work.[17]

By comparison, one study of the ICRC, noting its all-Swiss nature in the past, saw the organization in the following terms: it showed a commitment to liberalism aka human dignity, collective policy-making, emphasis on personal integrity and honesty, managerial expertise, transparent accounting, attention to detail, delay in accepting gender equality, aloofness, secrecy, legalism, aversion to public judgments, and "stolid public demeanor."[18] According to Peter Hoffman and Thomas Weiss, "[p]erhaps the ICRC best illustrates an institution's willingness to fundamentally reexamine its basic premises."[19] Instead of a rigid commitment to set tactics, the ICRC has been flexible in its own self-analysis, and, hence, more apt to make changes when necessary—albeit very slowly. This summary seems accurate since about 1970.

If we assume for the moment that this characterization is true, or mostly true, one of the more interesting questions is: what effects will the internationalization of staff and the promotion of non-Swiss individuals to high professional positions have on this traditional organizational culture? That is, if we accept for purposes of discussion that the ICRC has the organizational culture it now does largely because it has been a Swiss organization, not some other neutral nationality like Swedish or Irish, what will a different staff mean?

Will the ICRC be as dedicated to victims of war and politics, with such great determination and honesty, when the director-general is Belgian or Pakistani? Will the organization be as cautious and as averse to public statements when the director of operations is Canadian or Nigerian? Will there be debilitating conflict between the president and the director-general when the former remains Swiss but the latter is American? Will that projected situation damage the image of neutrality?

If we accept that some traits of Swiss political culture have been transferred to the ICRC during the time when the ICRC was all-Swiss,

What if the director is not Swiss?

what can we expect when much of the leadership is multinational? The answers to these questions are, of course, unknowable at the moment. Raising the questions, however, gives us a framework for looking at possible changes in the future. As of 2015, the professional staff has been internationalized for about twenty-five years, and the Directorate was indeed multinational. The ICRC contemporary organizational culture did not seem overtly affected by these facts. Just as some in colonial India became more British than the British, so non-Swiss nationals at the ICRC might adhere just as strongly to traditional organizational values as the Swiss there.

Notes

1 Organizational details of the ICRC are to be found in its Annual Reports.
2 Swiss neutrality arises out of both international and domestic considerations. Switzerland is a small state in the midst of more powerful neighbors. Also, Switzerland is made up of different linguistic and religious groups. Because of its domestic social composition, it is very difficult for Swiss citizens to agree on domestic and foreign policy issues. Hence Swiss neutrality in foreign affairs has been chosen as much for domestic political reasons as for foreign policy calculation.
3 Senator Jon Kyle chaired a Senate Republican policy committee that put out a "research paper" proposing the internationalization of the ICRC Assembly. Secretary of State Condoleezza Rice and other important Republican officials opposed the idea. The driving factor behind Kyle's actions was unhappiness with ICRC statements about US policy toward enemy detainees in the US "war" on terrorism. Some ultra-conservatives or super-patriots in Washington considered the ICRC to be just another left-wing, European organization with an anti-American bias.
4 We explain below that the professional staff was internationalized from the early 1990s. If this turns out well, and when the director-general and the rest of the directorate is non-Swiss, pressures may increase to internationalize the Assembly.
5 See the important analysis in Rainer Blaudendistel, *Between Bombs and Good Intentions: The International Committee of the Red Cross (ICRC) and the Italo-Ethiopian War, 1935–1936* (New York: Berghahn Books, 2005).
6 The Blaudendistel book, *Between Bombs and Good Intentions*, confirms the analysis in Jean-Claude Favez, *The Red Cross and the Holocaust* (Cambridge: Cambridge University Press, 1999). President Max Huber and other important members of the Assembly were deeply patriotic. Their commitment to Swiss nationalism caused them to appease both fascist Italy and Germany, at the expense of certain victims of war.
7 Stephanie Strome, "Red Cross Head Quits," *New York Times*, 14 December 2005, A-32. Jacqueline L. Salmon, "Red Cross Leadership at Issue," *Washington Post*, 30 December 2005, A-4. Even after some internal reforms, the ARC was still caught up in controversy about how it spent large sums of money in Haiti after the 2010 earthquake.

8 See especially Blaudendistel, *Between Bombs and Good Intentions, and Favez, The Red Cross and the Holocaust.*

9 See further David Forsythe, *The Humanitarians: The International Committee of the Red Cross* (Cambridge: Cambridge University Press, 2005).

10 This was in the late 1960s and early 1970s. See further Forsythe, *The Humanitarians.*

11 See the ICRC Annual Report for a detailed chart of this organization.

12 Peter J. Hoffman, and Thomas G. Weiss, *Sword and Salve: Confronting New Wars and Humanitarian Crises* (Lanham, Md.: Rowman and Littlefield, 2006), 174–75.

13 See Marcel Junod, *Warrior Without Weapons* (Geneva, Switzerland: ICRC, 1982); Arieh Ben-Tov, *Facing the Holocaust in Budapest* (Geneva, Switzerland: Henry Dunant Institute, 1988), André Rochat, *L'Homme à la Croix* (Vevey, Switzerland: Editions de L'Aire, 2005). Conventional wisdom holds that Rochat was an outstanding delegate in Yemen, but much less of a success as director-general for the Middle East. For a contrary analysis, see Blaudendistel, *Between Bombs and Good Intentions,* about how the ICRC did not have confidence in Sydney Brown in the Italo-Ethiopian War. This author also questions the record of Junod.

14 Blaudendistel, *Between Bombs and Good Intentions.*

15 Swiss banks, generally known for financial dependability and reliability, got a black eye for the way they handled Jewish property from the era of World War II, and for the way they dealt with that issue later. See especially Stuart E. Eizenstat, *Imperfect Justice: Looted Assets, Slave Labor, and the Unfinished Business of World War II* (New York: Public Affairs, 2003).

16 In general see Michael Barnett and Martha Finnemore, *Rules for the World: International Organizations in Global Politics* (Ithaca, NY: Cornell University Press, 2001), which treats these organizations as bureaucracies.

17 Gil Loescher, *The UNHCR and World Politics: A Perilous Path* (New York: Oxford University Press, 2001).

18 Forsythe, *The Humanitarians,* 240–41.

19 Hoffman and Weiss, *Sword and Salve,* 190.

3 The ICRC and international humanitarian law

- International law
- International humanitarian law
- Creating IHL: the Geneva Conventions and beyond
- Implementing IHL
- Emerging Legal Issues
- Conclusion

The ICRC has played a unique role in the development of international humanitarian law (IHL). It is not the only organization which has attempted to promote legal developments regarding humanitarian protection and human rights in armed conflict. The ICRC has, however, been a catalyst in the development of IHL dating back to the nineteenth century (1864), and is widely recognized as "the guardian of IHL," although there is much ambiguity about that role.

Typical ICRC activities for legal development include drafting articles for treaties, hosting meetings of legal experts, engaging in quiet diplomacy at international conferences, and articulating its view of the contents of customary international law for armed conflict. In the late twentieth and early twenty-first centuries, the ICRC has worked in conjunction with other actors such as the UN to enhance and modernize IHL.

Certainly in this domain the ICRC operates on the basis of state consent, because it is states that approve treaties in diplomatic conferences. With regard to customary international law, where state practice can morph into legal obligation to continue that practice, the ICRC recently sought state reactions to its views as it tried to clarify a rather murky subject. In a major undertaking, the ICRC legal division produced a massive compilation on contemporary customary IHL, then invited state reactions.[1]

This chapter discusses the evolution of IHL and the role played by the ICRC in furthering humanitarian protection in the legal realm. Beginning in 1864 and over the course of the twentieth century, the

ICRC quietly pushed for expanded legal protection for wounded soldiers, POWs, and civilians. We trace this development into the twenty-first century and conclude with the more recent attempts by the ICRC to limit human suffering caused by land mines. We also give attention to the role played by the ICRC in achieving a third protocol to the 1949 Geneva Conventions in 2005.

International law

International law refers to those conventions, treaties, regulations and customs developed by states to regulate behavior connected to international events. One of the main characteristics of international law (IL) is that it is state-centric. States are the actors that negotiate, formally approve, and otherwise establish IL. At times they do so with the help of non-state actors such as the ICRC. Under IL, states are the only entities that have full legal personality. Other actors, such as the United Nations, have only partial legal personality. In other words, they have some rights and duties, as determined by states, but not on a par with states. Other actors besides states may be liable under the law, such as those fighting for an entity not widely recognized as a state: "rebels," militias, national liberation movements, and so on. Individuals may also be legally accountable under IL, not just the collective we call a state. States may obligate themselves under IL for a variety of reasons, such as furtherance of reasons of state, desire to advance human dignity, and the wish to be associated with "public goods" such as the rule of law. But we are speaking of states, which in general have considerable power. That being so, it is difficult to deal with legal violations. As Geoffrey Best put it, "The prima-facie complaint about international law is simply this: that it holds together better on paper than in practice, and that states determined to ignore it can do so more or less with impunity."[2]

IL, unlike domestic law in many states, is accompanied by neither a police force nor a real system of courts with binding jurisdiction to enforce it. During the Cold War, when the Soviet Union invaded Hungary in 1956 and Czechoslovakia in 1968, how was one supposed to enforce IL without starting a devastating World War III? If we assume for purposes of discussion that the US invasion of Iraq in 2003 constituted illegal aggression, how was one supposed to change US policy? States do not usually allow disputes about the use of force to reach the World Court (International Court of Justice). Other courts do not usually have jurisdiction over such disputes either.

Some would go further and suggest that IL is impotent. Certainly until the 1990s, there were few instances of a national leader being held accountable for violations of IL, including IHL.[3] The conventional wisdom has been that IHL, dealing with the *process* of war, along with the law to regulate the *recourse* to force, comprises the weakest part of IL. When states and other armed actors are determined to use force, it is difficult to impose legal order.

International humanitarian law

IHL is an attempt to limit the devastation and horrors of armed conflict. It is an attempt to interject moral considerations into state calculation of self-interest in the quest to limit the conduct of war. As Hilaire McCoubrey explains, "IHL is, broadly that branch of public international law which seeks to moderate the conduct of armed conflict and to mitigate the suffering which it causes."[4] But David Kennedy reminds us that IHL codifies military necessity as well as concern for the individual.[5] Parts of IHL have more to do with state perceptions of narrow self-interest than human dignity. For example, fighters who do not wear uniforms and carry arms openly can be denied prisoner of war status, or ICRC visits to those detained in connection to war may be delayed because of military necessity.

IHL, or *jus in bello* for war victims, is based on separation from the law seeking to regulate the start of war, or *jus ad bellum*. The latter had its foundations in medieval Christian writers such as Augustine. Augustine (AD 354–430) believed that conflict and war were inevitable given the tendency of humans towards aggression and competition. Thus he articulated conditions when wars could be considered just. These revolved around notions of self-defense and a state's treatment of its inhabitants. If a state was attacked, the state was acting morally in defending itself. Likewise if a neighboring state was unjustly attacked by an aggressive nation, other states could fight a war to defend the vulnerable. Augustine saw this as defense of the innocent. Augustine also argued that a state that treated its own citizens inappropriately could be attacked to stop the injustice.[6] The ICRC has consistently avoided commenting on the justness of a war, and questions dealing with aggression and self-defense, instead choosing to focus on *jus in bello*.

Just as there are moral reasons for going to war, there were also moral ways to conduct a war.[7] Within IHL there are a few distinct traditions.[8] The two most important areas are the traditions of the Hague and Geneva (one could also add Nuremburg and individual responsibility to this list). Our emphasis will be on the development of Geneva (or Red Cross) law, focusing on victims.

First we offer a passing remark on Hague law. Developed in two conventions, the first in 1899 and the other in 1907, Hague law focused mainly on the methods and weapons employed during war (aerial bombardment for example, or illegal weapons like dum-dum bullets). This law, however, also paid attention not only to means and methods of warfare, but also to victims. Specifically, Article 4 of the 1907 Hague Convention IV set out the basic protection for POWs which would be developed more fully by the ICRC in 1929:

Prisoners of war are in the power of the hostile government, but not of the individuals or corps who capture them. They must be humanely treated. All their personal belongings, except arms, horses, and military papers remain their property.[9]

The Hague tradition focused on the obligations of states as they conducted wars.[10] The legal tradition arising out of the activities of the ICRC was Geneva law, focusing not on means and methods, but on victims. As noted in the second chapter, the creation of the committee which became the ICRC and ultimately led to the First Geneva Convention (1864), had its origins in the horrors of the Battle of Solferino. The ICRC would continue from then on to encourage greater protection for the victims of armed conflict as the need arose. A few important elements are essential to the 1949 Geneva Conventions (GC) and Additional Protocols, which comprise the most important part of modern IHL. We mention these core elements briefly here and elaborate on them further.

First, there is the combatant/non-combatant distinction. Those individuals not taking an active role in hostilities are not to be targeted or abused by those combatants who are fighting. This notion is absolutely central to contemporary efforts to limit war. Those, like Al Qaeda, who do not respect this principle, are essentially committed to total war rather than limited war to spare as many victims as possible. Second, fighters, when *hors de combat*, or out of the fight, are to be given a humane quarantine for the duration of the war. Third, those responding to the needs of victims, and their resources, are to be regarded as neutral. Thus, an ICRC offer of services is to be regarded as a neutral act, or a facility marked with the RC protected symbol (to be explained more fully later) is to be regarded as immune to attack. Another important distinction, produced more by states than the ICRC, is that between international armed conflict (armed conflict between two or more states), and non-international armed conflicts (armed conflict occurring within a state). International wars are covered by the bulk of IHL, while internal wars are covered by Common Article 3 in the 1949 law, and Additional Protocol II, in addition to whatever customary IHL exists on the subject. Violence such as riots and rebellions that do not rise to the level of armed conflict are not covered by IHL but rather by human rights law. IHL is one aspect of IL and shares in its weaknesses. There is no guarantee that individuals who violate IHL will be held accountable and punished. For example, the 1864 Geneva Convention established no means of enforcing that treaty.[11] At some points in the twentieth and twenty-first centuries, international courts have been established and individuals charged with violations of IHL. The Nuremburg and Tokyo tribunals, created in the aftermath of World War II, are examples of such courts. Although not without criticism, especially of victor's justice and prosecution for *ex post facto* crimes, Nuremburg and Tokyo were early blueprints for the international courts that followed: the International Criminal Tribunal for the former Yugoslavia (from 1993); the International Criminal Tribunal for Rwanda (from 1994); the International Criminal Court (from 1998). There have been other internationally approved criminal courts as well, connected to events in places like Sierra Leone, East Timor, Cambodia, Lebanon, etc.

Most of IL, in so far that it is adjudicated at all, is adjudicated in national courts. But national courts, whether military or civilian, are notoriously reluctant to apply rigorous legal justice to their own nationals in a situation of war. Historically states have been reluctant to establish strong enforcement mechanisms that could leave their citizens vulnerable to prosecution and restrict state sovereignty. The criminal courts noted above try individuals, not states.

Despite the historically limited effort to adjudicate international law connected to force, all governments and all state military establishments officially support legal regulation of force. In theory, they oppose aggressive use of force (part of *jus ad bellum*) and they support legal limits on the process of using force (*jus in bello*).

Creating IHL: the Geneva Conventions and beyond

The 1864 Geneva Convention

The First Geneva Convention developed out of a conference of states held in Geneva, Switzerland, in 1864. The Swiss government hosted the conference and invited mainly Western European states to discuss codifying assistance to wounded soldiers. It was the efforts of the

ICRC to publicize the importance of medical assistance in times of war throughout Europe that led to this diplomatic conference in Geneva. But ultimately the codification of IHL is a state-dominated process. In wartime it is states that allow medical provisions for soldiers, and it is states that sign international treaties. Despite the central role played by states, the ICRC was central to the 1864 treaty (it drafted the text), and for the Geneva law that developed thereafter. The essence and purpose of the 1864 Geneva Convention was to ensure that soldiers injured in battle would receive medical assistance, so as to prevent further suffering. So long as the soldier had laid down his arms, neutral medical assistance should be provided based solely on need.[12] The ICRC sought the establishment within each country of a private society to collect medical supplies in preparation for wartime and then assist those wounded. Hence, if a war broke out, the national society could provide medical assistance to those soldiers in need. The ICRC realized that state consent would be necessary for medical assistance to be carried out in proximity to the battlefield. Furthermore, the ICRC saw the need for the neutralization of the medical personnel providing assistance. To prevent these individuals from becoming a target, the ICRC sought to have them wear a distinctive sign, which was initially a red cross on a white background.[13] This too required state consent and a guarantee by a state's military not to attack any medical personnel wearing this protected emblem.[14] Ultimately 12 states agreed to these provisions and the first element of Geneva law was created. Dunant argued that the 1864 Geneva Convention was a "legal watershed with respect to efforts to reduce the suffering engendered by war."[15] By 1867 over 20 states had ratified the GC, including the Russian and Ottoman empires (although the latter insisted on the neutral emblem of a Red Crescent rather than Red Cross).[16]

The 1906 Geneva Convention

The 1906 Geneva Convention for the Amelioration of the Condition of the Sick and Shipwrecked Members of the Armed Forces at Sea tried to extend the basic protection found in the first GC to those military personnel fighting sea battles. Individuals serving in their country's navy were no less entitled to basic medical treatment than their counterparts on land. Thus, the ICRC lobbied for the creation and protection of medical vessels that would accompany their navy into battle. These floating hospitals, as well as their crew, were also to be granted neutral protection, as were medics assisting wounded soldiers on land. This presented some additional logistical problems for medical assistance but none that were insurmountable according to the ICRC. In pushing for the 1906 Geneva Convention, the ICRC saw the logical extension of the humanitarian protections found on land to sea warfare. Simultaneously, the 1864 Convention for land warfare was revised to take into account humanitarian issues not adequately covered by the earlier treaty.

The 1929 Geneva Convention

The 1929 Geneva Convention focused on providing humanitarian protection to prisoners of war (POWs). This developed in response to the conditions of World War I. World War I saw various abuses committed against captured military personnel. It was during the Great War that the ICRC expanded its "services" beyond wounded soldiers in battle to those soldiers who were POWs, despite the lack of a precise legal mandate. ICRC delegates made hundreds of visits to POWs held in military camps and provided food and supplies. Geneva even published the reports of its POW visits. Following these experiences, the ICRC began the push for enlarging IHL. Again we should note that the ICRC acted on the ground before more complete legal mechanisms were developed to protect vulnerable individuals. That is, while the earlier Hague Conventions from 1899 and 1907 mentioned POWs, the specifics of that law did not prevent the reprisals and appalling conditions that the ICRC witnessed in the POW camps during 1914–1918. From the perspective of the ICRC, there was little difference between the suffering of a wounded soldier on the battlefield and a captured soldier held in a military camp who lacked basic food or medical treatment. The basic principle was the same: protect the dignity of fighters *hors de combat*.

ICRC activities eventually led to the 1929 Geneva Convention for the Protection and Welfare of Prisoners of War. This treaty attempted to establish some fundamental rights for captured soldiers. POWs could not be tortured or assaulted, nor could they be paraded around or humiliated. The detaining power must provide for the basic needs of the POW including food, water, medical treatment, and housing. The treaty did not provide for ICRC rights of visitation; that was to come in 1949. Yet during World War II, states that had consented to the 1929 Convention generally afforded the ICRC access to POWs. This access is one of the most significant activities of the ICRC. Today the ICRC has more access to POWs and other categories of detainees stemming from violent situations around the world than any other organization.

The ICRC's activities and experiences during World War I demonstrated the need for the development of additional protections for other fighters and those seen as enemies in the eyes of a government. The situation in Hungary and Russia in 1919, and immediately thereafter, indicated to the ICRC that individuals detained in internal war or for political opposition were just as vulnerable to abuse as prisoners of war. Thus, the ICRC, after World War I, having expanded its practical work for POWs, also expanded its work on the ground for other fighters *hors de combat*, or those viewed as an enemy.

Furthermore, given the devastation and destruction of cities and the countryside during World War I, the ICRC recognized that civilians were more vulnerable than in past wars. The ICRC after World War I attempted to get legal protections for civilians caught up in armed conflict. However, because of governmental policies, it would have to wait another 20 years before this would come to fruition via the Fourth Geneva Convention of 1949 for civilians in war and occupied territory.

The four Geneva Conventions of 1949

The four GCs of 1949 remain the core of modern IHL. Despite a determined effort after World War II by the communist camp to discredit and even destroy the ICRC, the ICRC was essential to these legal developments.[17] The ICRC, acting with the Swiss government, saw a diplomatic conference convened, which resulted in the most significant and far-reaching development of IHL thus far. All states have now formally agreed to the requirements and obligations of the four interlocking treaties of 12 August 1949 for victims of war.[18] The intent of most of the four treaties is to humanize international armed conflict. To avoid complications from situations of undeclared war, Article 2 states:

> In addition to the provisions which shall be implemented in peacetime, the present Convention shall apply to all cases of declared war or of any other armed conflict which may arise between 2 or more of the High Contracting Parties, even if a state of war is not recognized by one of them.

The four GCs of 1949 incorporated many aspects of the previous conventions designed to protect fighters who were sidelined for various reasons, and extended basic humanitarian protection to civilians. For example building on the first Geneva Convention of 1864, but also reflecting some of the horrors of World War II, Article 12 of the First 1949 GC says of military personnel:

Wounded or sick, shall be respected and protected in all circumstances. They shall be treated humanely and cared for by the Party to the conflict in whose power they may be, without any adverse distinction founded on sex, race, nationality, religion, political opinions, or other similar criteria. … Any attempt upon their lives, or violence to their persons, shall be strictly prohibited; in particular, they shall not be murdered or exterminated, subject to torture or to biological experiment.[19]

The detailed protections laid out for POWs in the 1929 Geneva Convention were also reaffirmed and expanded. The 1949 POW convention (the Third 1949 GC) called for "the humane treatment of prisoners from the moments of capture and interrogation, through all facets of the internment, up to their return to normalcy through the gates of release, repatriation, or death."[20] The basic premise was that POWs should not suffer. As Rousseau had argued much earlier, upon capture, the POW ceased being an active agent of his (or her) state and reverted to being an individual citizen entitled to respect for human dignity.

According to the new fourth GC of 1949, civilians were to be protected from looting, from becoming a hostage, and from acts of violence against their person or property. Furthermore, civilians were entitled to food, water, and medical assistance from an occupying power. As the United States was to discover in the wake of its 2003 invasion of Iraq, a state seizing control of foreign territory by force had specific and extensive legal obligations to the civilian population. Or, one has the "Pottery Barn Rule": as Secretary of State Colin Powell said in the context of debate before that invasion, if you break it, you own it.[21] The ICRC's interest in protecting civilians stemmed from its experiences in the two world wars, as well as internal wars in places like Spain. The ICRC sought a fundamental distinction between the military (those fighting) and the civilian population (those vulnerable individuals taking no part in the armed conflict). This distinction is essential to IHL.[22]

Norms protecting civilians were not new concepts in the middle of the twentieth century. There existed a long tradition in various regions of the world of immunity for non-combatants. McCoubrey, for example, outlines humane treatment of civilians (and soldiers) in Indian history.[23] One could see the same thinking in notions of chivalry and religious mandates among soldiers during the Crusades. Women, children and the elderly or sick were considered vulnerable or in need of special protection.[24] Thus, in times of war, honorable soldiers would not target or abuse those vulnerable individuals they might come upon. Of course it is also true that despite notions of chivalry, religious obligations, or Enlightenment morals, in all wars, violence upon innocent civilians has occurred.

An additional area of concern for the ICRC was conflicts within a state or non-international armed conflict. International law and the previous Geneva Conventions focused on armed conflicts between or among states. States were reluctant to extend humanitarian protection and legitimacy to those trying to overthrow their government or carve out a new polity. Uprisings within states were viewed by state leaders as criminal activities. However, the ICRC saw little humanitarian difference between civil wars and international armed conflict. In the Spanish Civil War of the 1930s, one saw the participation of outside parties, such as the Soviets on the side of the Spanish republicans, and the Germans and Italians on the side of the Franco rebels. The internationalized civil war is not a new phenomenon. From the perspective of the ICRC, all that mattered was protecting human dignity, regardless of the source of that threat. This was legally accomplished by the minimal protections set out in Article 3, common to the four 1949 GCs. These protections would be refined and made more complex in Additional Protocol II in 1977.[25]

By the end of 1949 over 50 states had signed the four new GCs. By 2015 all widely recognized states had consented to the 1949 Geneva Law. The 1949 GCs were, according to Caroline Moorehead, "what the earlier ones had always been: a set of rules, against which could be made appeals for decent treatment during armed conflict."[26] They were, to paraphrase the Canadian public figure Michael Ignatieff, a firewall against barbarism. They were intended to guarantee that belligerents did not become barbarians. What was true of human rights law in the UN era was also true of IHL from 1949: states wanted to be seen as legitimate and civilized, and so they signed on to the law; but that was not the same as fully implementing the law in concrete situations.

The Additional Protocols of 1977

The ICRC, while not the primary force behind the Additional Protocols, did help to expand the Geneva Conventions and IHL. The ICRC assisted in drafting the protocols even though many states left their fingerprints on different articles in the two legal instruments.[27] Protocol I extended IHL in international wars, while Protocol II focused on internal wars. Protocol II, building on Common Article 3 from 1949, still remains the only treaty pertaining to internal armed conflict (but with a definition of that type of conflict somewhat different from Common Article 3).

Part of the drive for the Additional Protocols came from the newly created states of the Third World. Having emerged from the decolonization of the 1950s and 1960s, these states wanted international law and IHL in particular to reflect their interests. One specific aspect that they saw lacking in IHL was protection for those fighters involved in national liberation movements contesting colonial and imperial governments. Especially when looking at Protocol I, we see that many Third World states saw it as a means to target South Africa's apartheid government and Israel's occupation of Palestine. The Third World, supported by the communist camp, wanted Black South African and Palestinian fighters to have POW status and protection.

Box 3.1 Common Article 3

Common Article 3 states the minimal standards of humane treatment:

> In the case of armed conflict not of an international character occurring in the territory of one of the High Contracting Parties, each Party to the conflict shall be bound to apply, as a minimum, the following provisions:

1   Persons taking no active part in the hostilities, including members of armed forces who have laid down their arms and those placed hors de combat by sickness, wounds, detention, or any other cause, shall in all circumstances be treated humanely, without any adverse distinction founded on race, color, religion or faith, sex, birth or wealth, or any other similar criteria.

2   To this end, the following acts are and shall remain prohibited at any time and in any place whatsoever with respect to the above-mentioned persons:

  a   violence to life and person, in particular murder of all kinds, mutilation, cruel treatment and torture;
  b   taking of hostages;
  c   outrages upon personal dignity, in particular humiliating and degrading treatment;
  d   the passing of sentences and the carrying out of executions without previous judgment pronounced by a regularly constituted court affording all the judicial guarantees which are recognized as indispensable by civilized peoples.

3   The wounded and sick shall be collected and cared for.[28]

An interesting and significant aspect of the third and fourth GCs in 1949 for the ICRC was the inclusion of the right of visits to detained persons, whether military or civilian.[29] These two GCs obligated states to give the ICRC access to POWs, and detained civilians covered by the fourth GC.[30] Visits could be delayed, but not indefinitely, only by imperative military necessity, which, unfortunately, was not defined.

The basic attempt was to grant a higher legal status to "wars of national liberation," so they would be classified as an international war rather than some kind of "internal" violence. Thus, the development of this aspect of IHL was thoroughly wrapped up in power politics. Not surprisingly both Israel and the United States refused to ratify Protocol I.

An additional point to note concerning the Additional Protocols relates to the convergence of Hague and Geneva law. In the two Additional Protocols we notice articles that deal with traditional Geneva protections such as protection of civilians, detention conditions, and access to POWs. For example, API, Article 48:

> Parties to ... conflict shall at all times distinguish between the civilian population and combatants and between civilian objects and military objectives and accordingly shall direct their operations only against military objectives.[31]

API attempts to clarify the combatant/civilian distinction by arguing that anyone who is not a combatant (who is not taking active part in hostilities) is a civilian. The subject is not so simple as it might first appear. There is, factually speaking, the guerrilla or terrorist fighter who uses force but is not easily identified as such, being out of military uniform and sometimes posing as a harmless civilian. A number of governments view some irregular fighters as "unprivileged belligerents" who do not have the rights of regular military personnel when captured or otherwise made *hors de combat*. By comparison, the ICRC sees such individuals as entitled to humane treatment as civilians.

That is to say, the ICRC sees all individuals caught up in armed conflict as protected by IHL, whereas some governments see guerrilla fighters out of uniform, and certainly terrorists posing as civilians to carry out violent attacks, as lacking humanitarian protections. The ICRC does not argue for special protections for terrorists, only that as civilians they are not be tortured or treated cruelly and are entitled to minimal considerations of due process. The whole subject continues to roil debate about IHL and treatment, for example, of "terror suspects." This is especially perplexing because international law presents no definition of terrorism and does not clarify who might be a "terrorist." API also included requirements concerning the methods of combat. Thus, in the Additional Protocols we see the merging of Hague and Geneva law. This is not all that surprising given that the methods used in armed conflict (Hague tradition) will have an impact on injuries to soldiers/combatants and on civilians (types of weapons used, i.e. exploding bullets, chemical agents, etc.). Since the ICRC's primary concern is to protect human dignity in armed conflict, and since threats to human dignity can arise from various sources, it is understandable that the ICRC would eventually become the guardian and promoter of Hague law as well as Geneva law.[32] Moreover, one of the leading champions of Hague law at the turn of the century, the Russian czar, was no longer around.

It is worth reiterating that the ICRC was not the sole actor, nor lead actor in the development of the Additional Protocols. By the 1970s the ICRC was no longer the only organization interested in IHL. Given the role of the United Nations in international relations and the existence of numerous NGOs interested in human rights and humanitarian protections, the ICRC is now just one voice among many in the field. When compared to the 1864 Geneva Convention we see a very different international environment, and hence, it is not difficult to understand that the role of the ICRC in the development of IHL has somewhat diminished over time, or at least become more complicated.

To summarize major legal developments about IHL in 1977, one can say the following. First, newly independent or post-colonial states and their communist allies were successful in rewriting parts of IHL to emphasize wars of national liberation and their "freedom fighters," but this was accomplished at the cost of having the United States and some of its closest allies like Israel and Turkey reject API. To the latter, API was based on subjective and politicized concepts and was unworkable. Second, the developing countries, and indeed most countries faced with internal unrest, having gotten what they wanted in API, then were decidedly lukewarm about APII. Most newly independent or post-colonial states faced instability from internal ethnic and other divisions, as did older states like India. These states were not enthusiastic about further development of IHL that might restrict their policy choices in suppressing internal armed actors. Hence they insisted that APII apply only when, for example, rebel movements held sufficient territory over time to apply the terms of the Protocol—a difficult standard to reach in most contemporary civil wars (battle lines fluctuate and territorial control shifts).

So while there was much talk about humanitarian law and humanitarian values, the driving force at the 1974–1977 diplomatic conference was government calculation of self-interest. Many if not most governments prioritized how to advance their interests and impede the interests of their political opponents. API and APII existed. But the former was unacceptable to parts of the Western coalition, and the latter was much watered down, not universally accepted, and in fact almost never formally invoked in subsequent situations of violence.

However, all was not gloom and doom. In fact, various parts of the additional protocols found their way into national military manuals and other non-treaty documents that affected how military establishments operated. And various parts of the additional protocols were cited by this or that court, national or international. So the protocols did have some ameliorative effect on violent situations after 1977. It remained true, nevertheless, that IHL has seen no further general development via diplomatic conference. Both the ICRC, and the Swiss government that actually hosts such conferences, looking back on 1974–1977, have drawn the conclusion that states cannot be trusted to elevate a concern for human dignity over self-serving political maneuvers in such diplomatic conferences. As we will show, this does not mean that progress cannot be made on strictly limited subjects, like land mines or neutral emblems, that do not allow political maneuvers that might undermine existing IHL.

Land mine treaty: The 1997 Ottawa Convention on anti-personnel mines

Anti-personnel land mines were of particular concern to those interested in IHL because of the indiscriminate damage that can be done to non-combatants. Small anti-personnel land mines, triggered by body weight or a trip wire, while effective from a military point of view, could prove to be incapacitating or even deadly years after a conflict ended if they were not properly mapped and then deactivated. All too often land mines were not deactivated, and civilians who accidentally came upon them would suffer loss of limb or death by merely walking in the wrong field. The ICRC played an important role to limit the use of land mines via the development of the Ottawa Treaty. In this we see the ICRC adopting a more assertive role as a public advocate, while still avoiding finger-pointing in public about particular governments or other fighting parties.[33]

The ICRC encouraged the Canadian government to focus on limiting the use of these land mines. As President Sommaruga stated bluntly in 1995, land mines are "an affront to humanitarian values, an affront to civilization."[34] The ICRC tried to persuade other states to become involved in the issue by compiling data on the number of civilians hurt or killed after fighting ended. Based on ICRC activities over the years, these statistics lent authority to the subject. Furthermore, the ICRC engaged in a very public campaign for the land mine treaty by such measures as having military personnel testify against the weapon and enlisting the activism of well-known personalities such as the late Princess Diana of the United Kingdom. The United States, which was the ICRC's largest donor, pressed the organization to abandon its support for a total ban on anti-personnel mines. The United States was prepared to accept a ban on "dumb" mines but wanted to keep legal the "smart" mines that could be electronically deactivated. President Sommaruga resisted this pressure, stood firm for a total ban, and was backed by the ICRC Assembly. Thus, the ICRC joined with other NGOs and many national RC societies, along with "like-minded" states, to achieve the Ottawa Treaty. The Ottawa Convention establishes a total ban, forbidding "the production, stockpiling, use, and export of anti-personnel landmines."

This ban was fundamentally humanitarian in purpose.[35] The United States has not, ratified this treaty as of 2015, arguing that anti-personnel land mines are militarily necessary in places like the Korean peninsula. Over 160 states have consented to the treaty, although some states have not, like China, Russia, Iran, and North Korea. In President Obama's second administration, building on the US record of being the most generous donor to international de-mining efforts, he initiated studies about how the United States might move to accept the treaty. This was a surprising but slow process and did not bind his successor.

Despite a complicated and broad legislative process for modern IHL, in this case the ICRC carved out a special place for itself in the campaign leading up to the Ottawa Treaty. It lent its authority in IHL to the process, helping to dispel the notion that those in favor of the ban were radicals and amateurs.

The 2005 third Additional Protocol

The ICRC was also important in the legislative process that added a third protocol to the 1949 GCs, this time on the subject of neutral emblems.

The ICRC had long been trapped in a controversy primarily involving Israel. The 1949 GCs, formally created by states, recognized the Red Cross and the Red Crescent on a white background as neutral symbols in armed conflict. Israel and its official aid society, Magen David Adom (MDA), refused to use either one, but rather the red Star of David (six-sided star). Therefore, under its rules and the rules of the RC Movement, the ICRC could not recognize MDA as part of the RC network. That being the case, the RC Federation could not admit MDA to membership. The ICRC was sometimes falsely accused of being anti-Semitic and biased against Israel. These charges, however false, were not helpful to its work, especially after the controversy about whether the ICRC had tried hard enough to help Jews under Nazi control in the 1930s and 1940s.[36]

To complicate matters, the leadership of the American Red Cross (ARC) started withholding its assigned dues to the core budget of the Federation, in protest over the exclusion of MDA. The fact that the Federation could not admit a society that had not been previously recognized by the ICRC seemed to make no difference to the ARC. And the fact that the ICRC could not recognize a society that had not agreed to use a neutral emblem approved by states also seemed not to matter to the ARC. So the Federation lost about 25 percent of its core/administrative/headquarters budget on an issue over which it had no control. Given this situation, and given ICRC quiet discussions with several key governments interested in this question, early in the twenty-first century the ICRC took up a new round of diplomacy to resolve the impasse. The result, to make a long story short, was the calling of a diplomatic conference by the Swiss government in late 2005, and the adoption, by divided vote, of a "Red Crystal" as a third neutral emblem. The RC Movement then met in June 2006 and adopted the same third emblem in its proceedings, thus allowing for the recognition of MDA, which agreed to use the new symbol in its international operations. MDA was then recognized by the ICRC and admitted to the Federation. States voting against the Red Crystal, led by Syria, were mainly Arab and Islamic. For them the issue was the legitimacy of the state of Israel, and recognition of its quasi-governmental aid society in international relations. Again we see that interest in RC humanitarianism can get entangled in power politics. But again we see that the ICRC was central to legislative developments on IHL, working quietly with a variety of governments and national RC societies, and certainly working with the Federation, to finally resolve this sticky problem that had aroused various passions.

Implementing IHL

Having played a role in drafting aspects of IHL, the ICRC is also engaged in efforts and activities to see that IHL is respected and implemented during armed conflict. Most of what we have to say on this matter is treated in the chapters that cover provision of assistance and relief, detention visits, and tracing of missing persons.

Here we briefly note that to begin to see IHL respected, it first must be known. For example, in Somalia in the 1990s, it was only a slight exaggeration to say, as some did, that no one with a weapon had ever heard of the GCs. Similar problems confronted ICRC delegates some 30 years earlier in the violence that engulfed Yemen. The Yemeni fighting parties, with the exception of Egypt, then fighting on the side of the Yemeni Republic, had never heard of IHL or the RC Movement, much less the ICRC.[37] Thus the ICRC and national RC societies now hold workshops and seminars, and in myriad ways, from comic books to puppet shows, try to disseminate the principles and basic notions found in IHL.

It is crucial that the military within a state understands its obligations under IHL. Thus, servicemen and women must receive proper training in the content of IHL, and especially the GCs. Given the lack of adjudication, historically, on behalf of IHL, the law has been generally applied to the extent that it has through military training and supervision. In other words, given the historical absence of hard law through court decisions, IHL has been mostly implemented through the soft law of military training. It has been said of the My Lai massacre in Vietnam (1968), in which Lt. Calley and others killed hundreds of unresisting and unthreatening civilians under their control, that many US conscripts had been rushed into the violent situation without adequate training in the laws of war.

Dissemination is an obligation of the GCs (1949). For example, Article 144 of the Fourth GC specifically requires states to spread the norms of IHL.[38] The norms of Additional Protocol I covering issues of criminal justice place the emphasis on commanders to properly train, supervise, and control their subordinates.

Emerging Legal Issues

Even as existing IHL proved difficult to implement, the ICRC was hard at work on trying to ensure that the law kept up with new technologies. Drones and cyber war were two such developments. (Space does not permit a discussion of autonomous or robotic weapons that once activated can engage targets on their own without further human control. These kinds of weapons raised serious and complex questions for IHL.)

Unmanned aerial vehicles, commonly called drones, could be weaponized and employed for remote killing. Drones could hover over an area for a considerable time and with advanced cameras watch for enemy activity. Operators half a world away could launch missiles to destroy a target. Hence US military personnel, sitting in a secure facility in Missouri or Nevada, could carry out a military strike in Pakistan or Yemen, for example. Israeli security officials sitting in Israel proper could do the same in Gaza.

On the one hand it was claimed that drone warfare allowed more control, more precision, and more timely proximity for legal advisors. On the other hand it was argued that drone warfare had intentionally targeted persons who were not really combatants, had led to much collateral damage by the unintended killing of civilians, and had been used in situations that were not really characterized by armed conflict. Politically speaking, it was also argued that the heavy use of drones in places like northwest Pakistan or Gaza had inflamed the local population, who resented constant surveillance and sudden attack.

The ICRC engaged with various parties on the subject, seeking to clarify both old and new legal rules that might apply to drone warfare. The ICRC well understood that effective regulation in this area would depend on state acceptance. It therefore sometimes sought to clarify options for future rules, noting that existing IHL was not constructed with drones in mind. At the same time, the organization did not hesitate to advocate for certain traditional IHL principles that seemed relevant—e.g., the duty to distinguish between combatants and civilians, the duty to exercise prudence in making that distinction, and the duty to follow the rule of proportionality in deciding when and how to act.[39] Impeding clear rules were the facts that much information in this domain remained classified, and that the lack of full reciprocity meant that states possessing weaponized drones seemed in no hurry to agree on new IHL restrictions.

Techniques of cyber warfare also drew the organization's careful attention. In the organization's view, "Cyber warfare refers to operations against a computer or a computer system through a data stream, when employed as means and methods of warfare. Cyber attacks against transportation systems, electricity networks, dams and chemical or nuclear plants could have devastating consequences."[40] There was widespread agreement that future armed conflict among developed states would certainly involve extensive cyber warfare. Already in peacetime, various states were penetrating foreign computers and data systems, certainly for purposes of spying and maybe for purposes of embedding malware that could be activated in future armed conflicts. The ICRC's concern with the humanitarian consequences of computerized warfare does

> "not mean that IHL applies to any cyber operation or to all those that are often called 'cyber attacks' in common parlance: IHL does not regulate cyber operations that fall outside a situation of armed conflict. Business corporations and governments are as much concerned by cyber espionage, cyber crimes, and other malicious cyber activity as they are by cyber attacks that would fall under IHL. The technical means of protecting cyber infrastructure from espionage or from an attack might be similar, but the law governing these operations is not. One of the key issues is therefore to identify the circumstances in which cyber operations may be regarded as occurring in the course of armed conflict, or giving rise to armed conflict in and of themselves, such that IHL would apply."[41]

The above view gives rise to an important question. If we assume for purposes of discussion that the United States and Israel infected certain Iranian computerized systems in about 2009 with a virus (Stuxnet) to impede the possible development of an Iranian nuclear weapon, did such a move constitute a use of force regulated by IHL? If one could destroy a potential weapons system, or a dual use system (civilian and military) by electronic means instead of explosive/kinetic means, was the former equivalent to use of force? What was the difference between the 1981 Israeli military (kinetic) attack on an Iraqi nuclear facility, and its 2007 military (kinetic) attack on a Syrian nuclear facility, compared to the alleged Stuxnet event? Logic aside, what we can say about actual events was that no state at the time of Iranian computer malfunctions in its nuclear energy research in about 2009 claimed that use of force had occurred. That might not be true in similar situations in the future. In 2008 in the context of an armed conflict between Russia and Georgia, the latter was hit by a cyber attack that disabled its internet. Apparently that was part of the Russian use of force. By 2015 the United States was warning China publically about cyber attacks on American computer systems that appeared to emanate from buildings controlled by the Chinese military.

In general, the ICRC's position with regard to cyber warfare was similar to its view of drone warfare. It argued that while some new rules might need to be developed for an updated IHL, more so for cyber warfare compared to drones, some traditional IHL principles applied automatically—such as distinction, precaution, and proportionality. The ICRC was looking ahead, fearful about the consequences for civilians and civilian infrastructure, and being proactive in trying to get states to limit the destructiveness of future hi-tech warfare.[42]

Conclusion

The ICRC, as guardian of IHL, tries to advance a legal framework to limit the destruction of war, whether international or internal. At the same time, to prioritize its field work involving relief to the civilian population, detention visits, and tracing of missing persons, it tries to minimize its role in public accusations about which fighting party has violated which aspect of IHL. It will sometimes make such public pronouncements, but only as a last resort. The ICRC, therefore, walks a delicate line, a balancing act on a high wire as it were, between emphasizing the legal obligations of states and other fighting parties under IHL, and getting on with its services to the victims of war. Some of these humanitarian services require discretion and prudence instead of public accusations.[43]

Notes

1 *Customary International Humanitarian Law*, www.icrc.org/eng/resources/documents/publication/pcustom.htm.
2 Geoffrey Best, *War and Law Since 1945* (Oxford: Oxford University Press, 1994), 5.
3 Slobodan Milosevic, before his death, was one of the few national leaders to be brought before an international court. He was indicted in connection to war crimes, crimes against humanity, and genocide. He was not indicted for waging aggressive war or any other charge relating to *jus ad bellum*. We explain this latter concept below.
4 Hilaire McCoubrey, *International Humanitarian Law* (Brookfield, Vt.: Ashgate Publishing Company, 1998), 1.
5 David Kennedy, *The Dark Sides of Virtue: Reassessing International Humanitarianism* (Princeton, N.J.: Princeton University Press, 2004).
6 A brief but early statement for humanitarian intervention. Augustine, *Political Writings* (Indianapolis, Ind.: Hackett Publishers, 1994).
7 Although it is worth noting that in most instances military necessity will trump IHL in its various forms.
8 One may argue that there is quite a bit of overlap between the different traditions and therefore these distinctions are not so clear cut. We would agree, and as will be shown at the end of this chapter, the ICRC has been active in the development of Hague law as well as Geneva law. However, at this point in the chapter it is best to describe these distinct traditions and then show how they have converged.
9 McCoubrey, *International Humanitarian Law*, 24.

10 Hague law would eventually come under ICRC aegis, but at the end of the nineteenth century Hague law was not part of the ICRC's focus. The ICRC played no role at the 1899 and 1907 Hague conferences.

11 John F. Hutchinson, *Champions of Charity: War and the Rise of the Red Cross* (Boulder, Colo.: Westview Press, 1996), 53.

12 McCoubrey, *International Humanitarian Law*, 79.

13 See our discussion later regarding the ICRC and neutral symbols.

14 Unfortunately this legal protection via neutral emblems has not always been foolproof. All too often during the twentieth century individuals working for the ICRC have been deliberately targeted and killed. For example, six RC workers were intentionally killed in Chechnya in 1996.

15 Caroline Moorehead, *Dunant's Dream: War, Switzerland and the History of the Red Cross* (New York: HarperCollins, 1999), 46.

16 Moorehead, *Dunant's Dream*, 52.

17 Particularly Moscow was incensed that the ICRC had not done more to help Soviet POWs in Nazi hands, although the Soviet Union had not ratified the 1929 GC. In general, Moscow viewed the ICRC as very close to the Swiss government, which was not wrong, and as part of the capitalistic West that was hostile to the Soviet Union and its allies. Moscow therefore organized an attack on the ICRC, using principally the various socialist RC societies. This was much in evidence during the Korean War that started in the early 1950s. The Soviets did not cooperate with the ICRC in the run-up to the 1949 GCs.

18 Advisory Source on IHL, 07/2004. www.icrc.org.

19 McCoubrey, *International Humanitarian Law*, 81–86.

20 Best, *War and Law Since 1945*, 135.

21 David Samuels, "A Conversation with Colin Powell," *The Atlantic*, (April, 2007), www.theatlantic.com/magazine/archive/2007/04/a-conversation-with-colin-powell/305873/.

22 Best, *War and Law Since 1945*, 115. One way to protect civilians was to set up non-military zones which combatants would agree to respect. Unfortunately states did not see the value in these neutral zones and have not established these zones in most instances. In the Balkan wars of the 1990s, the UN declared certain "safe areas" but did not provide the effective military forces to defend them.

23 McCoubrey, *International Humanitarian Law*, 9.

24 Best, *War and Law Since 1945*, 25.

25 McCoubrey, *International Humanitarian Law*, 26–27.

26 Moorehead, *Dunant's Dream*, 557.

27 The ICRC was a bit reluctant on the Additional Protocols, fearing that states might weaken IHL and hence this diplomatic conference would be a setback.

28 International Committee of the Red Cross, *The Geneva Conventions of August 12, 1949* (Geneva, Switzerland: July 1970), 76.

29 "An impartial humanitarian body, such as the ICRC, may offer its services to the Parties to the conflict." Best, *War and Law Since 1945*, 178.

30 Best, *War and Law Since 1945,* 155.

31 McCoubrey, *International Humanitarian Law*, 177.

32 Even prior to the 1970s the ICRC had ventured into Hague territory. In 1918 the ICRC criticized the use of poison gas and later helped to see the

1925 Poison Gas Treaty codified. As shown below, in the 1990s the ICRC would also be active in developing the treaty to ban anti-personnel land mines.

33 McCoubrey, *International Humanitarian Law*, 50.
34 Moorehead, *Dunant's Dream*, 707.
35 Ramesh Thakur and William Maley, "The Ottawa Convention on Landmines: A Landmark Humanitarian Treaty in Arms Control?" *Global Governance*, vol. 5, no. 3 (July/Sept 1999), 273–302.
36 Just as the Ottoman empire started using the Red Crescent in the 1870s, so the Pahlavi government in Iran started using the Red Lion and Sun for its official aid society. This latter development was never endorsed in IHL, but states and the RC Movement deferred to this *fait accompli*. The Iranian RC society was allowed to be a part of the RC Movement. Israel and MDA were definitely treated differently from the Iranian case. After the Islamic revolution in Iran in 1979, the Iranian RC society adopted the Red Crescent, and use of the Red Lion and Sun ceased. The ICRC did not withdraw recognition from the Iranian RC society when it used the Red Lion and Sun. The ICRC has never withdrawn recognition from any RC society. In the various wars in the Middle East, a number of Arab and/or Islamic parties respected the MDA emblem in practice—e.g. not attacking its ambulances marked with the Red Star of David. In relative terms, field activities were less controversial than diplomatic conferences. The ICRC had working relations in the field with MDA—and also the Palestinian Red Crescent, also for a time unrecognized because the Palestinian RC was not part of a state that had become a party to the 1949 GCs.
37 See the fascinating memoir by André Rochat, *L'Homme à la Croix* (Vevey, Switzerland: L'Edition Aire, 2005).
38 McCoubrey, *International Humanitarian Law*, 67.
39 Jelena Pejic, "Extraterritorial Targeting by means of Armed Drones: Some Legal Implications," *International Review of the Red Cross*, May 2015, www.icrc.org/en/document/jelena-pejic-extraterritorial-targeting-means-armed-drones-some-legal-implications. She was writing in her personal capacity.
40 ICRC, "Weapons: ICRC statement to the United Nations, 2014," www.icrc.org/en/document/weapons-icrc-statement-united-nations-2014#.VMDDbuktDcs.
41 ICRC, "What limits does the law of war impose on cyber attacks?," www.icrc.org/eng/resources/documents/faq/130628-cyber-warfare-q-and-a-eng.htm.
42 Cordula Droege, "Cyber warfare, international humanitarian law, and the protection of civilians," *International Review of the Red Cross*, 94, 866 (Summer 2012), 533–578. www.icrc.org/eng/assets/files/review/2012/irrc-886-droege.pdf.
43 For an explanation of how the ICRC prioritizes services to victims of political violence and seeks to avoid public commentary on specific war crimes and other matters of controversial international criminal law, see David P. Forsythe, "The International Committee of the Red Cross and Access to International Justice," in Patrick Keyzer, *et al.*, eds, *Access to International Justice* (London and New York: Routledge, 2015), pp. 178–188. In effect, the ICRC prioritizes social justice, in the form of its services to victims, over legal justice in the form of criminal law, in its own policies.

4 Humanitarian assistance and restoration of family ties

- The notion of humanitarian assistance
- The Nigerian Civil War, 1967–1970
- The Balkan wars, 1991–1995
- Somalia, 1991–1994
- Conclusion

The International Committee of the Red Cross started with a focus on wounded fighters and also showed early interest in detained fighters, but from World War I on it also focused on civilians. From a moral point of view, why should a concern for victims of war be limited to combatants but not civilians? As military technology evolved, so did the numbers of civilians in distress from fighting—from such factors as aerial attack and long-range bombardment. Because of these technological and other reasons (e.g. ethnic cleansing), modern wars in places like the Balkans resulted in victims that were about 85 percent civilian.[1] Thus, for both material and political reasons, many modern wars tended to be total wars, with great civilian destruction. While some ICRC assistance is directed to wounded or otherwise incapacitated fighters, most assistance is for the civilian population.

In the 1930s the ICRC, based on its earlier experiences, pushed for greater legal protection of civilians from the horrors of war. Unfortunately for civilians, these efforts were opposed by many states. It was not until 1949, after the great destruction of World War II, that states agreed to the fourth Geneva Convention of that year covering civilians in armed conflict and during occupation. While the overall treaty covers international war, Article 3 pertains to internal or intranational war. That Article provides that "Persons taking no active part in the hostilities ... shall in all circumstances be treated humanely ..." To this end, in particular certain acts were expressly prohibited, including "outrages upon personal dignity, in particular humiliating and degrading treatment." These standards pertained to civilians as well as to fighters who were *hors de combat* by wounds, sickness, or capture.

Under the fourth Geneva Convention there is a right to humanitarian assistance for the civilian population victimized by war, although the ICRC has no monopoly on the provision of this assistance.[2] The treaty, unfortunately, does not specify exactly who is to provide this assistance or under what conditions. The legal framework was not much clarified by Protocol I of 1977. While that addition to IHL reaffirmed a right to humanitarian assistance in armed conflict, it also failed to specify the details of that right. Yet, fighting parties are under a legal obligation to allow such assistance to civilians in need. This is the law on the books, which is often not fully matched by the law in action, mainly because of the policies of fighting parties.

In many wars, complex emergencies, and situations of internal troubles, the provision of civilian relief has become a central feature of the conflict, for both humanitarian and political reasons.[3] This was very true of the Nigerian Civil War (1967–1970), involving claims to independence by Biafra. It was equally true of the Balkan wars (1991–1995), involving the disintegration of former federal Yugoslavia. It was equally true in Somalia in the early 1990s, which descended into clan-fighting in the absence of a central government. In these wars, the ICRC was centrally involved, not least for reasons of trying to provide assistance to the affected civilian populations. In these and many other situations, the ICRC was at the center of the politics of humanitarian assistance.

The notion of humanitarian assistance ３ ways

The ICRC's humanitarian assistance is but a subset of the larger notion of humanitarian protection. The ICRC seeks to protect human dignity in conflicts by three primary means: development of international humanitarian law (IHL), detention visits, and assistance, mostly to civilians. This assistance, or relief, includes provision of food, water, clothing, shelter, and health care. It also includes restoring family contacts through the tracing of missing persons, restoration of other family ties, and a variety of other civilian-related tasks such as reintegrating former child soldiers into civil society. Increasingly some emergency civilian relief spills over into longer-term development assistance. For example, in some war-torn areas, the ICRC helps with the vaccination of cattle or the provision of seeds for planting, in order to help the civilian population become economically self-sufficient after debilitating conflict. So in the "hand off" from relief to development, the ICRC has developed a transitional role.

In moral terms, assistance operations are just as important as detention visits. "Protecting a person from death by starvation is just as important as protecting a person from death by torture. Protecting a person from hypothermia is just as important as protecting a person from confinement in painful positions."[4] In legal terms, the fourth Geneva Convention of 1949 for protection of civilians in armed conflict and occupation is just as important as the third Geneva Convention of 1949 for protection of combatants who are *hors de combat* (out of the fight).

The general process

ICRC assistance, mainly to the civilian population, can be analyzed according to five factors.[5]

Knowledge and access

First, the ICRC has to be aware of civilians in distress because of conflict and negotiate access to them. Because of the organization's numerous regional, national, and sub-national offices around the world, which serve as a basis for its extensive ongoing operations, the ICRC is usually well informed about the plight of civilians in international wars, civil wars, and internal troubles. Moreover its headquarters in Geneva not only keeps up with the international communications media but is in constant touch with diplomatic missions in Geneva and also a great variety of NGOs that have offices in that city. The ICRC circulates to its officials a daily review of the global press emphasizing humanitarian matters. The organization also, as a UN observer, has an office in New York through which the ICRC is in touch with virtually all members of the United Nations.

While the ICRC, because of IHL, has a right of detention visits in international war, it has no clear right to deliver humanitarian assistance in any of the various types of conflicts that can endanger civilians. But the organization normally "offers its services" to fighting parties, stressing its traditional work based on the principles of independence, neutrality, and impartiality. In many, if not in most, situations where the ICRC desires to activate its humanitarian assistance, it achieves some access—but not always to its full satisfaction. At a maximum it seeks freedom of movement to make assessments, the monitoring of relief to ensure neutrality and impartiality, administrative control over the delivery system for the same reasons, and the ability to implement studies that assess the impact of its relief.

On rare occasions it will find its relief at an end when the parties prevent a sufficient degree of neutrality or impartiality. This the ICRC discovered in the 1980s regarding Ethiopia. That government had adopted a relocation scheme for civilians, designed to significant degree to deprive enemy irregular fighters from using normal civilian life as a cover for their military operations. For the ICRC to provide civilian assistance in relocation camps was to provide support for one of the basic strategies of the Ethiopian side. Since the ICRC was not able to negotiate alternatives to its satisfaction, it either withdrew or was asked to leave, depending on which unclear report one wishes to believe. The point is that the organization strives for its relief to be seen as both impartial (equal concern for all in need) and neutral (not unreasonably contributing to the political or military objectives of a principal party).

Its preferred mode of operation is to proceed only on the basis of the negotiated consent of the parties. There are legal and other reasons for this: the ICRC is linked to IHL as approved by states, and throughout its history it has tried to nurture the good will of public authorities— which presumably allows the organization to achieve what it does. A practical fact looms large, however, in such considerations. It is very dangerous, if not impossible, to organize a large-scale relief effort in secret or against the wishes of a fighting party. The ICRC operates on the principle of neutrality, which means that in theory, and in fact 99 percent of the time, it does not allow any weapons in the vicinity of its operations. So the ICRC normally negotiates the terms of its access for its unarmed relief efforts. In the last analysis, it is all too often the fighting parties with their weapons that control the extent of, and nature of, humanitarian relief.

In virtually all modern conflicts, the ICRC has achieved some degree of access to civilians in distress. This was true in Palestinian territory occupied by Israel after the 1967 war (and complicated by other violence in that area after that time), in Cambodia after the Vietnamese invasion of 1979, during the Balkan wars of the 1990s, in Somalia during the early 1990s, in Rwanda during 1994, and so on through the conflicts in the Sudan (Darfur), the Democratic Republic of Congo, and Syria and South Sudan, which were continuing at the time of writing. The ICRC was there in the midst of conflict, and much of its work was devoted to civilian assistance of various sorts. During World War II, the ICRC normally provided relief *after* combat, in occupied territory for example. Since the Nigerian Civil War, the ICRC normally operates *in the midst of conflict*, as well as in occupied territory.

Sometimes it becomes too dangerous for the ICRC to deliver relief in conflicts, and so in modern conflicts in places like Bosnia and the

Democratic Republic of Congo, it has had to suspend its operations for a time.

In a few situations the ICRC undertook a "cross-border" relief operation without the advance consent—or clear consent—of one of the fighting parties. It might have informed such a party of its operations at some point in time, but it did not secure clear consent in advance. This has occurred as far back as the Nigerian Civil War (1967–1970), along the contested border between Ethiopia and Eritrea and Tigray in the 1980s, and in that same decade along the Iranian-Iraqi border during their long war (1980–1988). In the Nigerian case, a Red Cross relief plane was eventually shot down by elements of the Nigerian air force, with loss of life, contributing to the termination of the ICRC role in that conflict. In the Ethiopian case, Red Cross relief trucks were fired upon by elements on the Ethiopian side, but ineffectually. These and a few other cases of "cross-border" operations constitute the exceptions that prove the general rule that the ICRC normally proceeds with relief on the basis of the negotiated consent of the parties.

In the Syrian internationalized internal armed conflict that began in 2011, the UN Security Council at one point authorized cross-border relief into rebel-held territory without the consent of the Syrian authorities. But the ICRC was not involved in this. It did carry out some relief in rebel held areas, but under truces and other arrangements negotiated with the fighting parties. Its relief actions took place mostly in government-controlled areas. The ICRC worked extensively with the Syrian Arab Red Crescent, which despite being chartered by the government, displayed considerable independence and was accepted as a legitimate humanitarian actor by various fighting parties. As a result of its leading role in humanitarian relief, over forty SARC staff have been killed in relief operations as of 2015. The ICRC had several of its staff taken hostage by various militants but has not experienced the casualty rate of its RC partner.

Assessment

Second, the ICRC must accurately assess civilian needs. The organization has personnel who specialize in this task and who can be dispatched on short notice from Geneva if they are not already in the conflict area. The ICRC prefers to make its own assessments, but at times it will rely on certain reliable partners. In Iraq during the mid-1990s, when UN-authorized economic sanctions had led to great hardship for the civilian population, the ICRC relied at least partly on assessments of the situation from the World Health Organization (WHO) and also UNICEF.

In many situations in the past, assessment of civilian need was a multifaceted and fragmented affair, with different organizations, sometimes including states, making partial reports based on their partial knowledge of different parts of the area affected. From the early 1990s the United Nations tried to improve on this state of affairs, and by the time of writing one found in New York an Emergency Relief Coordinator with the rank of Under Secretary-General. One of the roles of this office was to coordinate the various assessment reports from WHO, UNICEF, World Food Programme, the UN Development Program, etc., as well as the reports from various relief and development NGOs. The ICRC, while stressing its formal independence from the UN, cooperated with this system in a practical way. In addition to this network in New York (the NGO component was called InterAction), the ICRC stayed in close contact with a similar network of IGOs and NGOs in Geneva (the NGO component of which was ICVA). Because the ICRC is usually present in one way or another in most conflict situations, and because of its detailed and bottom-up process for planning each year's budget for the organization, the ICRC's assessment of civilian need is usually an important component of the larger system of assessment. Since at the end of each year ICRC delegations in the field have to make a projection of coming expenditure in the next year, the ICRC is constantly making assessment of the anticipated need for and cost of assistance to the civilian population. Not all such needs can be fully anticipated. There are always unanticipated invasions or collapses of order. But in general, ICRC assessment of needed relief is not a huge or chronic problem in most situations.

Mobilization of resources

Third, on the basis of knowledge and assessment, proper resources have to be mobilized in sufficient quantity.

The ICRC is well positioned to mobilize resources for relief, being part of widely respected international movement, having a legally recognized role in armed conflict, and being well known to the major donors such as USAID and the European Union's Humanitarian Office (ECHO). But the scale of disasters can exceed ICRC capability, the agency has not always mobilized certain types of relief, and it has not always proved adept at raising concern.[6]

The ICRC puts out an annual appeal for funds to deal with anticipated problems, as part of the UN-coordinated system of appeals. To this it adds emergency appeals as particular conflicts break out or evolve. These appeals go mainly to states and to RC societies. Responses are voluntary.

As we already documented, the main contributors to the ICRC are Western states, with the United States providing more or less 30 percent of ICRC resources. Other Western governments, including the EU, follow. Western Red Cross societies are also important donors, but they and their colleagues in the Federation provide only about 15 percent of the ICRC budget. Wealthy non-Western states, such as the Arab oil-producing states, have never been major donors to the ICRC regular budget, although most of them are quite familiar with the ICRC, and several among them—e.g. Kuwait, Jordan—have benefited from ICRC services. They sometimes contribute to special appeals or special programs in important ways.

The ICRC's budget expanded rapidly after the Cold War, given the various crises that erupted in the 1990s. With the demise of European communism and the global struggle between East and West, "humanitarianism" became more important—at least in the policies of "Northern" states.[7] Yet, even as the ICRC's overall expenditures moved into the range of $600–650 million per year, this was "small potatoes" given civilian need in places like the Balkans, the Great Lakes region of Africa, Sudan, the Democratic Republic of Congo, Iraq, Afghanistan, etc. As we already noted, $600 million was what the two US presidential candidates spent on advertising in the 2004 election.[8] Yet this was the approximate amount of the ICRC's annual budget in 2005, which was supposed to cover most of its humanitarian work around the world.

Sometimes the ICRC has been crucial to directing the world's attention to the need for humanitarian assistance, as in Iraq in the mid-1990s and Somalia in the early 1990s. Sometimes this has been done by persistent public and private diplomacy—as in the case of Iraq, for example. Sometimes this has been done by extraordinary action—for example in Somalia, where the ICRC took journalists at its own expense into rural Somalia to see first-hand the extent of civilian suffering, so that reporting in the Western-based communications media could spread the word.

At other times the ICRC record has been less impressive. It was somewhat slow to respond to the need for assistance in the violence in the Balkans in 1991. There, eventually it welcomed an increased role for the Office of the UN High Commissioner for Refugees (UNHCR) because civilian need was outstripping its capacity to respond.

Ironically given its start, the ICRC for a time did not much emphasize mobilizing medical relief. Despite Henry Dunant's initial focus on medical relief to the war wounded, for a long time the ICRC largely left to others, both states and national Red Cross and Red Crescent societies, the job of medical relief. This was in part because modern military establishments developed state-of-the-art medical divisions. But with the founding of Doctors Without Borders in the early 1970s, and with the prevalence of civil wars in developing countries featuring one or more fighting parties with no or poor medical services, the ICRC renewed a more vigorous mobilization and coordination of this phase of assistance. Particularly commendable, on the other hand, has been the ICRC's emphasis on the importance of potable water for civilian welfare in conflicts. In Iraq, for example, from 1991 and thereafter, and certainly during the 2003 invasion, the ICRC delegation featured outstanding work by water engineers and other water experts, which was of great value to the civilian population, especially in several major cities.

To protect the dignity of war victims through provision of relief, one has to start with proper water and sanitation systems.

Deliver a ch ug

Fourth, the ICRC is normally one of four major relief actors in the actual provision of assistance in conflicts. The others are the UNHCR, UNICEF, and the World Food Programme.[9] In places like Cambodia around 1980, the ICRC, despite being a private organization, teamed with UNICEF to manage a very large relief program. It acted on a par with UNICEF, and in some ways was more dynamic than UNICEF. In Bosnia during the early 1990s, it was second only to the UNHCR in the size and importance of its relief operations. In Somalia at approximately the same time, it was the most important relief actor in that failed state, keeping alive millions through its improvised and dangerous efforts.

In large crises, the ICRC knows that needs will exceed even its best managed response, and so the organization has cooperated more and more with other relief agencies. In the past the organization had developed a certain reputation for being difficult to deal with and somewhat isolated. Perhaps it had developed a very high opinion of itself and its roles. But these traits changed considerably as much chaos after the Cold War showed the need for systematic partnership among aid agencies. For example, in Rwanda in 1994, the ICRC concentrated on tasks within that country that had been wracked with civil war and genocide, while leaving to the UNHCR and its partners the response to the flight of several million persons into neighboring states. The ICRC often arrived at an amicable division of labor with UNHCR and other relief agencies.

Both had overlapping mandates. The UNHCR came to focus on war refugees as part of its operations. But war refugees, as civilian victims of war, also fell under the traditional focus of the ICRC. The ICRC had been dealing with refugees in a major way since at least 1919, whereas the UNHCR was created in 1950.

Given the different situations relief actors face, having a flexible relief system with different lead actors can be a good thing.[10] In some conflicts like in Somalia, the ICRC may be best positioned to be the lead agency for the international community in responding to civilian need. In other conflicts like Bosnia, the UNHCR may be best positioned. In still other conflicts, it may be UNICEF. Flexibility has much to be said for it.

Moreover, in any conflict in contemporary times, as a matter of fact somewhere around 200 relief NGOs may become involved. Many of these have impressive credentials and capabilities, like Oxfam or CARE or Save the Children. Many of them sub-contract with the UNHCR, or perhaps with USAID, and become part of an official public program. Still others like World Vision, a faith-based relief and development agency with excellent contacts in Washington, have good records of action in particular countries.

What unites many of these NGOs is acceptance of a code of conduct for relief personnel in international operations.[11] Many NGOs now accept in fact large parts of the ICRC's operating principles. The code, written first by the ICRC and Federation, consists of 10 points:

1   the humanitarian imperative should trump politics;
2   aid is to be impartial and based on need;
3   aid is to be neutral and not for religious purposes either;
4   relief agencies should strive not to act in behalf of governmental policy;
5   those agencies should respect culture and custom;
6   they should build local capacity where possible;
7   the beneficiaries of relief should be involved in the management of relief;
8   relief should pay attention to future vulnerabilities;
9   relief agencies should be accountable to both beneficiaries and donors; and
10   victims should be seen not as objects but as dignified humans.

There remains some debilitating duplication, overlap, and competition. ICRC relief efforts in Cambodia about 1980 were sometimes undercut by Oxfam. ICRC relief efforts in Ethiopia were sometimes undercut by the Federation. Both Oxfam and the Federation wanted more of "the action," more "market share," at the expense of the ICRC's efforts on behalf of neutral and impartial relief.[12]

Overall, the ICRC has a well-deserved reputation for rapid and dependable relief action in contemporary times. This will be shown by several case studies later in this chapter.

Evaluation and planning

Fifth, since the time of the Nigerian Civil War, the ICRC has recognized the essential need for evaluation and planning in place of amateurish and ad hoc decisions. It has a policy evaluation unit within the professional side of the organization. The Assembly and its Executive Council review the actions of the director-general (the equivalent of a prime minister) and the Directorate (the equivalent of a cabinet). The organization utilizes outside consultants on management and policy questions. There is an outside audit as well as several from inside. The annual budget making process also serves as a policy planning exercise. The organization not so long ago did a broad-based review of its strategy and tactics.[13] Summary reports about assistance (and other subjects) are presented to the Red Cross Conference. The ICRC participates in a variety of meetings and workshops and planning exercises with the Federation and those NGOs and IGOs involved in relief, both in New York and Geneva.

These five factors in ICRC assistance programs can be seen at work in the following case studies. The Nigerian Civil War is included because of its importance to the organization; it shows the dangers of amateurish policy-making. The case studies of Bosnia and Somalia show how even carefully considered relief policies can encounter dangers and obstacles in the brutal conflicts after the Cold War. The three together show how the ICRC has become more professional about relief, which is to say more careful about systematic policy making. The three case studies also show how dangerous relief work can be in the context of callous and self-serving public authorities. Often it is clear that humanitarian relief programs are not for the faint of heart.

The Nigerian Civil War, 1967–1970

When Biafra declared its independence from Nigeria in 1967, based mostly on a sense of disaffection by the Ibo people as fueled by the political ambitions of leaders like Lt. Col. Ojukwu, the ICRC certainly knew about the situation and negotiated a certain role for itself. The

negotiated a rule

story was prominently covered in the North Atlantic press. Britain, the former colonial power in what became Nigeria, and the United States tilted toward the government in Lagos and its leader Gen. Gowon. France (and Portugal) tilted toward Biafra, if only to offset Anglo-Saxon influence in Africa. An ICRC delegate, Georg Hoffmann, was experienced and capable. With keen European interest in the conflict, in part stimulated by Biafran public relations consultants there, the ICRC dispatched Aguste Lindt to be its special representative. Lindt was experienced in humanitarian affairs, having been head of UNHCR. He came to be the primary policy-maker for the ICRC in that conflict.[14]

Humanitarian assistance to the Biafran people soon emerged as the most salient issue to outsiders in this conflict. Given public and governmental interest in the situation, the ICRC had no trouble mobilizing considerable assistance based on the assessments provided by Hoffmann and Lindt. Both Western governments and Red Cross societies provided the goods, services, personnel, equipment, and money needed for a major relief effort. The ICRC, however, did not have the assistance field to itself. The French Red Cross, closely linked to the French government, operated separately from the ICRC and its partners—the latter drawn mainly from circles that included the British and Nordic Red Cross societies, but also those from Finland and Switzerland. There was also Joint Church Aid, a Western ad hoc faith-based consortium of relief NGOs. The latter tended toward solidarity with Biafra, not being much interested in nice notions of Red Cross neutrality. Negotiating clear access as well as the actual delivery of relief proved not only problematic but actually deadly. Biafran leaders understood that images of starving civilians in the Western press were useful for political purposes. Charges of genocide against Lagos fueled independence policies by leaders like Ojukwu, who would be recognized as head of a sovereign state if Biafran independence became a reality. Biafran authorities also arranged for flights carrying weapons to be mixed in with relief flights by various parties. So Biafra was in no hurry to reach agreement with the Federal side in Lagos about a neutral land corridor for relief to Biafran civilians. For Ojukwu, whatever distress "his" people were enduring, adequate civilian relief would undermine his short-term and long-term political objectives.

For the Federal side, Gen. Gowon insisted that under the principles of IHL, which he agreed to respect even though this conflict was from his view a civil war, a fighting party had the right to inspect and supervise relief to the rebel area, to guarantee there was no contraband. It was a fact that Biafra was using relief flights to slip in weapons. But Biafra would not agree to relief that started from Federal territory, because such a process would reinforce Federal claims to sovereignty over the Biafran area.

So both sides viewed relief primarily in political terms, and particularly Biafra sought to use relief issues to buttress its hard and soft power—the flow of weapons and sympathy in the international community.

The ICRC, based in pro-Biafra Europe, and competing particularly with Joint Church Aid for "market share" in delivering relief, negotiated a deal with Gen. Gowon that it could deliver relief flights to Biafra at its own risk. But on 5 June 1969, Nigerian air force fighter jets shot down a relief flight under contract to the Swedish Red Cross and part of the ICRC-organized relief effort. This incident proved fatal both to the crew and to the ICRC's involvement in the conflict. Lindt had been dynamic to the point of appearing brusque and insensitive to the Federal side. He was declared persona non grata by Lagos, and after August 1969 the ICRC delivered no more relief in the conflict.

Several facts proved salient after the fact. First, ICRC headquarters had proved incapable of developing appropriate strategy and tactics for the conflict. The Assembly was inattentive and amateurish, lacking a consistent plan or proper oversight. It delegated too much to Lindt on the ground, who proved more assertive than diplomatic, and who lost the confidence of Lagos. Hoffmann, more experienced in African affairs and more diplomatic, had been pushed aside. Second, the ICRC as an organization paid too little attention to IHL and its principles concerning neutral relief. Caught up in competition with JCA, it paid too little attention to the norm that belligerents had the right to supervise relief to guarantee its neutrality. It tilted toward Biafra, was manipulated by Ojukwu and other Biafran leaders, and paid too little attention to the efforts at reasonable relief by Gowon and the other Federal officials. The ICRC was unwilling to recognize the implications of Red Cross neutrality. If the parties could not agree on neutral relief, the ICRC's hands were tied. So it pushed ahead, until the Nigerian air force forced a halt.

After this conflict, the ICRC changed its headquarters arrangements to diminish the role of the volunteer Assembly and create more organizational governance by the new director-general and other professional managers. Also after the conflict, Bernard Kouchner, who had been active in the French Red Cross, created Doctors Without Borders (Médecins Sans Frontières), and later Doctors of the World. He and his colleagues were unhappy about the limitations imposed by the notion of Red Cross neutrality. He wanted a relief organization that could do good on the ground, but that would also speak out against civilian distress and other violations of human rights and humanitarian norms. He wanted active solidarity with "victims," not neutrality. Finally, after the conflict, when the Biafran secessionist movement had been defeated, there was no genocide against the Ibo people, but rather the eastern section of Nigeria was peacefully reintegrated into Federal Nigeria. Ojukwu later became a politician running for office in Nigeria.

The Balkan wars, 1991–1995

After World War II, Federal Yugoslavia was constructed as a multi-ethnic or multinational state, largely held together by the iron grip of Josip Tito. His dictatorship permitted a number of civil rights, especially in the cultural realm as compared to the political. There were also some freedoms entailed in "economic democracy," or worker participation in economic decision-making. But Tito did not permit freedom of speech and policy-making on behalf of the major ethnic or national groups within the state: Croats, Slovenes, Serbs, Albanians, Montenegrans, and those living in Bosnia and Herzogovina. These ethnic or national differences were simply suppressed. By the end of the Cold War only some 25 percent of the inhabitants of Federal Yugoslavia identified themselves primarily as Yugoslavs.[15]

With Tito's death in 1980, and after a period of uncertainty and instability, assertions of Serb nationalism came to the fore. These were championed by Slobodan Milosevic, who sought to advance his own political fortunes by leading a movement for "Greater Serbia." But greater power for Serbs meant less power and more danger for the other groups in Federal Yugoslavia. In the face of the "fantasy" of the virulent exceptionalist Serbian movement led by Milosevic,[16] Croatia and Slovenia declared independence in 1991. Bosnia and Herzogovina, with Sarajevo as its capital, and the most culturally and ethnically integrated of the federal republics, eventually followed suit.

Brutal fighting broke out, particularly between Serbs and Croats (who had tried to slaughter each other during World War II) and between Serbs and Bosnians. Many of the latter identified themselves as Muslim. Eventually, in the second half of the 1990s, Serb extremism turned against the ethnic Albanians in the region of Kosovo. Albanian Kosovars were also largely Muslim, as compared to the Orthodox Christianity of most Serbs.

Early ICRC role

The ICRC was not caught unawares by the downward spiral of events in the Balkans during 1990–1991. Although heavily engaged in other

international obstruction

parts of the world at this time, especially in Somalia, the organization had good contacts with various interlocutors in old Yugoslavia. It was already active on matters pertaining to "political prisoners." Moreover, it knew of various political circles because of long-standing contacts through the RC Movement. Because of its own position, plus coverage of events by the European communications media, the ICRC was aware of growing civilian need, and what was needed, as the 1990s progressed. So the organization was generally well positioned when fighting broke out between Serbia and Croatia in the Vokovar region of eastern Slovenia, in 1991, and slightly later between Serbia and Bosnia throughout that region.[17]

Especially in Bosnia, much fighting appeared to be between ethnic Serbs, Croats, and Bosnians of Muslim belief. But Serbs in Belgrade were behind much mischief on the part of Bosnian Serbs, and Croats in Zagreb similarly supported Bosnian Croats. Muslim Bosnians drew support from various Muslim "jihadists" coming from several foreign countries. In the Balkans in the 1990s, what was an international war and what was an internal war, and what might be an internationalized civil war, was not so easy to discern. This factual situation created some confusion about what parts of international humanitarian law applied. While the ICRC was somewhat slow in mobilizing civilian relief,[18] the real problem for the organization lay in the obstruction and treachery of virtually all parties to the fighting. These "warriors without honor"[19] did not hesitate to attack civilians. A central goal of the Serbs and Croats was to create ethnically pure territory, and thus they often found the ICRC's impartial and neutral humanitarianism a barrier to their desires. Even the Bosnians, who represented an ethnically mixed party to the conflict, and who had certainly not initiated the tensions and fighting, did not hesitate to violate humanitarian standards. The Bosnian leader Alija Izetbegovic, the Serb leader Milosevic, and the Croat leader Franjo Tudjman, all came under investigation for violations of international criminal law. Probably only the natural deaths of Tudjman and Izetbegovic prevented their joining Milosevic as defendants at the International Criminal Tribunal for former Yugoslavia (ICTY).

So the major problem for the ICRC was in the intentional obstruction of the delivery of humanitarian assistance to the civilian populations of the Balkans on a neutral and impartial basis, particularly in eastern Croatia and Bosnia. The fighting parties signed numerous humanitarian agreements, many of which were brokered by the ICRC. Unfortunately, most of these turned out to be worth less than the paper they were written on. The word of warriors without honor meant little.

In 1992 the same problem afflicted the United Nations High Commissioner for Refugees (UNHCR), which became the lead agency for civilian relief for the United Nations, on behalf of the larger international community. The ICRC welcomed this role for the UN refugee agency and worked out a friendly division of labor with it in the Balkans. UNHCR relief convoys were delayed, obstructed, and attacked, and in this respect there was little difference between the ICRC and UNHCR.[20] They both strove for impartial and neutral humanitarian assistance, which blocked the ethnic cleansing desired particularly by the Serbs and Croats. But some of the attacks on the ICRC and UNHCR may have come from Bosnian parties who wanted Western intervention on behalf of their cause, and who were not completely unhappy about atrocities which were covered by the Western media and which could be blamed on other parties.

A large part of the core dilemma was that Western donor states wanted to give the appearance of doing something about the violence in the Balkans while avoiding a decisive military commitment that would stop the fighting as well as stop the civilian atrocities. So, the United States and the states of the European Union wanted UNHCR and ICRC relief to continue, despite the difficulties. When Sadako Ogata, head of the UNHCR, suspended UNHCR relief to demonstrate the difficulties the organization faced, the Western states pressured the UN secretary-general, Boutros Boutros-Ghali, to order Ogata to resume UNHCR relief. She did so, and the relief efforts resumed.[21]

An additional problem faced particularly by the European states, was that a number of their citizens were deployed in the United Nations Protection Force (UNPROFOR), the UN security operation. It was dangerous to try to get tough with the fighting parties when they had the option of taking hostage Western "peacekeepers," lightly armed, on the ground in the Balkans. The Serbs in particular did not hesitate to utilize this option from time to time, knowing that it was mostly useful in keeping the Western states from effectively pressuring them about blocking the delivery of humanitarian relief.

Core ICRC dilemma

In the Balkans from 1992 to 1995, the ICRC's role as a neutral humanitarian intermediary was greatly restricted by the political strategies of the major protagonists. The Serbs and Croats wanted to expand their territory and power while purging the land they controlled of other ethnic groups. The Bosnian leadership wanted Western sympathy and eventually intervention to offset the policies of the Serbs (both the Serbs of old Yugoslavia and the Serbs of Bosnia). So the Bosnian leadership, like the Biafran leadership, actually found much of the civilian suffering useful to the political cause. The Bosnian leadership slowed the resumption of water supplies to Sarajevo for precisely that reason. Meanwhile, the Western states, until 1995, hesitated to put decisive pressure on the fighting parties because of fear of "another Vietnam," or of getting deeply involved in a long and costly conflict not involving their vital national interests. In the words of US Secretary of State Baker in the George H. W. Bush Administration, the United States had "no dog in this fight" in the western Balkans.[22] In the view of the early Clinton administration, the Balkans constituted a "problem from hell" that should be mostly avoided.[23] (American deaths in Somalia in 1993, in the context of a humanitarian relief operation, created domestic problems for the Clinton Administration in responding to civilian need both in the Balkans and in Rwanda.)

In the Balkans the fighting parties pretended to give cooperation, and the Western states pretended to give support, but the ICRC, like the UNHCR, was left without powerful partners in attempts to aid the civilian populations affected (and detainees, for that matter). The UNHCR ran the largest relief program, and the ICRC had the second largest, but they both faced the same obstacles. The fighting parties mostly fought a total war that was disdainful of limits on violence. These fighting parties, many of which were also involved in various black market activities, did not respect civilian immunity from attack, and did not respect a humanitarian quarantine for detainees. In the Balkans from 1992 to 1995, as in Kosovo later in 1999, the policies, especially of the Serbs, may have added up "only" to ethnic cleansing rather than genocide, in that the purpose of the policy was "only" to expel the opposing group rather than to destroy it. Be that as it may, such a policy was contradictory to the ICRC attempt to assist the civilian population where it was.[24]

In May of 1992, Frederic Maurice, head of the ICRC delegation for Bosnia, was killed when his relief convoy, clearly marked with the Red Cross, came under attack. All fighting parties had been notified of, and had not objected to, this relief mission. No party claimed responsibility for the attack, and no one was ever held legally liable. This event shut down ICRC operations in that area for a considerable time, as well as striking fear in those running UNHCR and NGO relief operations. The ICRC eventually resumed relief work, but without any change in the fundamental and frustrating situation.

Finally in 1995, after the massacre at Srebrenica, the largest in Europe since World War II, and after extensive Western media coverage of

larger states stayed out — ICRC had a hard time acting)

continuing atrocities, the United States took the lead in: (a) applying military and political pressure against the Serbs; and (b) mediating the Dayton Accords, which brought an end to that stage of the fighting, along with the resulting atrocities.[25] This was the type of political solution that the ICRC had been calling for in general, even as its commitment to Red Cross neutrality prevented it from lobbying for any particulars.

Resulting ICRC reports, mostly unofficial, stressed the weakness of the organization when faced with brutal interlocutors.[26]

ironic that they needed a state to step in

Somalia, 1991–1994

Somalia, emerging from colonialism as a patched-together state consisting of former British and Italian possessions, descended into murderous clan-fighting in the early 1990s. The central government, under Siad Barre, disintegrated after unwise domestic and foreign policies, and no domestic faction proved strong enough to replace it with any far-reaching power, much less authority. The Soviet Union and the United States had, from time to time, supported or opposed Barre, but with the end of the Cold War, each lost interest in Somalia. No outside actor, whether African or otherwise, had much influence with the various armed militias that fought among themselves and terrorized the local civilian population.[27]

Early phase

The ICRC, on the scene because of its interest in prisoner affairs, was one of the first organizations to sound the alarm about the plight of the civilian population. So again the ICRC was well positioned on the ground and in the know about events in Somalia. Despite the death of one of its Belgian expatriates, the ICRC stayed in the country to try to deliver humanitarian assistance, in addition to trying to continue with its attempts to protect those taken prisoner.

Courting assiduously the Western communications media with their capability of presenting the story of Somalia in Western political circles, the ICRC finally facilitated coverage by the BBC, CNN, the *New York Times, Le Monde,* and others. This was done, in part, by escorting journalists, at ICRC expense, into the rural areas where civilian starvation was most pronounced.

Other actors were also trying to direct more attention to Somalia, including UN Secretary-General Boutros-Ghali (who was originally from Egypt). During 1992 the UN responded with both a relief

facilitated coverage

operation and a security mission, but neither was able to deal adequately with widespread civilian suffering, malnutrition, and starvation, or with the rampant disorder. By the midsummer of 1992, the ICRC was reporting that 95 percent of Somalis were showing evidence of malnutrition, with 70 percent showing severe malnutrition.[28]

Central phase

In late 1992, US President George H. W. Bush authorized, with UN Security Council approval, a large-scale military deployment to ensure the delivery of relief, mainly that of food assistance, to Somalia. This policy was continued by the incoming Clinton Administration during 1993.

The ICRC was a key component of this major relief mission, as it had the best network for distribution of food in rural Somalia. It had stayed in-country during the worst of the clan violence, even when most of the other IGOs and NGOs had withdrawn. Whereas other relief agencies like the UNHCR and the World Food Programme had retired to the sidelines, the ICRC and a few others like the United Nations Children's Fund (UNICEF) stayed on. The ICRC had built up the Somali Red Crescent as a reliable and neutral partner.

For the first time in its history, the ICRC took the decision to operate as part of a military mission, because that was the only way, in the view of the top decision-makers of the organization, that widespread starvation could be checked in Somalia. Previously the ICRC had required even military transports carrying its relief goods to be weapons-free, even as the organization then turned around and hired local security forces to guard its facilities and resources on the ground. But in Somalia the ICRC finally developed a close partnership with an internationally approved military force, although in reality it was overwhelmingly a US militarized supply chain.

During the remainder of 1993 this arrangement largely halted, then reversed civilian starvation in Somalia. At times in 1993, 1994, and thereafter, the ICRC had to move its expatriate personnel to neighboring Nairobi, Kenya, because of a wave of kidnappings for ransom. But even from there, the ICRC managed to run relief convoys into Somalia, locally managed by reliable Somali partners, identified as such with the help of the Somali Red Crescent. The system worked, in that relief continued to be reliably delivered to those in need, with payment made to secure bank accounts in Kenya. The various militias did not consistently interfere with this relief system, in part because other militias working with the ICRC would exact their own sanctions for any interference.

None of this was previewed by IHL, but all of this demonstrated the creativity and pragmatism of the ICRC on behalf of the usual principles of impartial and neutral humanitarianism.

Later phases

The United States had always maintained an independent strike force in and around Somalia that was entirely separate from whatever military forces were approved by the United Nations, and sometimes composed of truly international or multinational forces. In short, these US Delta and Ranger forces were not part of the UN field mission called United Nations Operation in Somalia (UNOSOM I) or UNOSOM II. When, in the fall of 1993, this independent US strike force, on the basis of its own decisions, attempted a "snatch and seize" operation in central Mogadishu, in an effort to decimate the leadership of the Aideed faction, a large firefight resulted. In addition to 18 US military deaths, many Somali deaths resulted. This incident fore-shadowed the end of major international political involvement in Somalia, which occurred during 1994.[29] The Clinton administration, under growing congressional and popular pressure, basically ended its policy, approved by the UN, of coercive nation-building.

This event created the diplomatic "Mogadishu line": namely, that when Western support for humanitarian assistance crossed the Mogadishu line, and resulted in even a few casualties that could not be explained in terms of narrow self-interest, the international humanitarian mission could not be sustained.

Such events left the Somali civilian population to its fate, and at the time of writing in 2015 only a weak central government had been restored, propped up by a small UN military presence. On the other hand, while food shortages and some malnutrition persisted, widespread starvation did not return. Clan violence, while still in evidence, did not return to the murderous levels of 1991–1993. The ICRC was still active in Somalia as of 2015, focusing on civilians dislocated by sporadic violence as well as by drought. The ICRC paid great attention to water supplies and irrigation schemes. This work was as much a developmental effort as it was emergency relief. The organization continued with its other traditional duties, including tracing activities and support for hospitals and clinics.[30]

Because of continuing attacks and kidnappings directed toward the expatriate community, the ICRC continued to base its personnel in Nairobi, with periodic visits inside Somalia. As in certain other places, the ICRC found it prudent to remove the Red Cross emblem from its vehicles.[31] Rather than providing security from attack, the emblem had become a target for attacks.

The violence spilled over into Kenya, as Al Shabab, an Islamic militant group, used violence to "punish" Kenya for its support of UN efforts to create a moderate central government and stability for Somalia. The United States, unlike in the early 1990s, saw its security interests involved, as well as those of friendly Kenya. Al Shabab was one of several Islamic militant groups whose primary concerns were local but who were decidedly anti-Western and anti-United States. Washington feared that some persons of Somali heritage but with US passports might turn out to be terrorists trying to strike the American homeland. So once again the ICRC was operating in a complex political environment in which the fate of victims of war and instability was far from being the priority of self-interested governments.

Conclusion

The ICRC distinguished itself in Somalia in the early 1990s.[32] It displayed the creatively pragmatic fieldwork for which the organization has drawn plaudits over many years. In fact, its historic decision to work directly with US armed personnel in UNOSOM I broke the back of rampant starvation from late 1992 to late 1993. Its continued work of humanitarian assistance in Somalia up to the time of writing continues to show the ICRC commitment to impartial relief based on need, regardless of whether or not Western capitals and/or the United Nations decide to adopt policies of major engagement.

Tracing and restoring family contacts

The tracing of missing persons can be related to prisoner affairs, but it has broader significance as well. Sometimes when persons are missing, they are in fact detained by public authorities. Thus at times they may be "forcibly disappeared" and in the possession of a detaining authority who intentionally refuses to confirm facts. Obviously, establishing their existence in prison is the first step to securing their protection, either under humanitarian or human rights standards. This aspect of tracing is discussed further in the next chapter on detention visits.

Other missing persons are separated from family by natural disaster, war, refugee flight, or some other reason unrelated to imprisonment. In the wake of the Russian Revolution of 1917, for example, the ICRC delegate Woldemar Wehrlin helped Swiss citizens in Russia to send messages to their families, which provided reassuring information on their safety.[33] To give another example, the ICRC was invited by the American Red Cross to help trace missing persons after Hurricane Katrina in 2004.

The ICRC has shown persistent efforts in the tracing of missing persons. As early as 1870 the organization set up a tracing service in Basel in connection with the Franco-Prussian War of that year. The focus was on soldiers. Since World War I and its efforts in behalf of POWs, its tracing efforts have become a principle feature of its protection efforts. This was certainly so during World War II. The 1929 and 1949 Geneva Conventions provide detailed regulations about the right of POWs to communicate with family, subject to reasonable security control by the detaining authorities. Gitmo prisoners in the US War on Terror were allowed to send messages to family via the ICRC, even though from 2002 until mid-2006 the US government claimed that no part of the 1949 GCs covered such prisoners. By 2015 as some 112 prisoners remained at Gitmo, the ICRC had arranged video messaging between detainees and their families.

ICRC experience in tracing was reflected in the decision after World War II (in 1955) to put the organization in charge of the International Tracing Service in Bad Arolsen, in Germany, whose primary purpose is to "collect, classify, preserve and render accessible to directly concerned individuals, the documents relating to Germans and non-Germans who were interned in National Socialist concentration or labour camps, or to non-Germans who were displaced as result of the Second World War."[34] Today, the main activity of this center largely relates to insurance, inheritance and property claims of persons victimized by Nazi policies in the 1930s and 1940s. Historians, however, have much interest in the facts contained in the Arolsen records, and a decision has been taken in principle to open the center for general scholarly research that goes far beyond matters of private claims and settlements. Certain states control the center, with the ICRC serving as administrator. As of 2015, the ICRC has given up this managerial role, believing that the work of the center is only rarely related to pressing humanitarian concerns.

After the massacre at Srebrenica, Bosnia, in 1995, the worst atrocity in Europe since World War II, the ICRC headed an international group charged with the tracing of missing persons. The massacre by Serbian paramilitaries during the Balkan wars, and later efforts to cover up the crime (such as the covert digging up and moving of bodies), have made definitive determinations of death difficult to establish in many cases. In this situation and others, the ICRC itself does not engage in exhumations of bodies, but leaves such forensic work to other organizations like Physicians for Human Rights. In the case of Srebrenica, as of 2015 many of the missing had yet to be accounted for.

In places like Angola between 2002 and 2004, the ICRC, working with local partners, arranged the exchange of over 190,000 messages among family members. It also confronted the problem of children separated from their families and managed to reunite 600 of 1,500. The ICRC also addressed the problem, in Angola and elsewhere, of the reintegration of orphaned children, and child soldiers, into society after combat.[35]

Today the ICRC maintains a website where individuals can report missing persons and ask for an ICRC tracing effort.

Notes

1 International Federation of Red Cross and Red Crescent Societies, *World Disasters Report* (Geneva, Switzerland: Federation, various years).

2 Ruth Abril Stoffels, "Legal Regulation of Humanitarian Assistance in Armed Conflict: Achievements and Gaps," *International Review of the Red Cross*, no. 855 (2004), 515–46.

3 The term "complex emergency" has no legal standing. It came into usage at the United Nations to facilitate international action in a situation where one of the fighting parties, mainly the government, did not want to acknowledge that an internal armed conflict existed, but might agree to cooperate with international involvement as long as some non-legal term was used to refer to the exceptional situation.

4 David P. Forsythe, *The Humanitarians: The International Committee of the Red Cross* (Cambridge: Cambridge University Press, 2005), 168.

5 See further David P. Forsythe, "The International Committee of the Red Cross and Humanitarian Assistance: A Policy Analysis," *International Review of the Red Cross*, no. 314 (October 1996): 512–31. More generally see Larry Minear and Thomas G. Weiss, *Mercy Under Fire: War and the Global Humanitarian Community* (Boulder, Colo.: Westview, 1995).

6 Forsythe, "The International Committee of the Red Cross and Humanitarian Assistance: A Policy Analysis."

7 Philippe Ryfman, *La question humanitaire* (Paris: Ellipses, 1999).

8 Forsythe, *The Humanitarians*, 4.

9 In general see Andrew S. Natsios, *U.S. Foreign Policy and the Four Horsemen of the Apocalypse: Humanitarian Relief in Complex Emergencies* (Westport, Conn.: Greenwood Press, 1997).

10 See further Larry Minear, *The Humanitarian Enterprise: Dilemmas and Discoveries* (Bloomfield, Conn.: Kumarian, 2002).

11 "The Code of Conduct for the International Red Cross and Red Crescent Movement and NGOs in Disaster Relief," *International Review of the Red Cross*, no. 310 (1996), 55–130.

12 See further Forsythe, *The Humanitarians*.

13 This was the "Avenir" project. See ICRC press release 97/36, 16 December 1997.

14 One of the best treatments of the ICRC and the Nigerian war remains Thierry Hentsch, *Face au Blocus: La Croix-Rouge internationale dans le Nigeria en guerre (1967–1970)* (Geneva, Switzerland: HEI, 1973). Hentsch had privileged access to information because of his connections to Jacques Freymond, then acting president of the ICRC. One of the better sources in English remains John de St. Jorre, *The Nigerian Civil War* (London: Hodder & Stoughton, 1972).

15 Michael Ignatieff, *The Warrior's Honor: Ethnic War and the Modern Conscience* (London: Vintage, 1999), 41.

16 Misha Glenny, *The Fall of Yugoslavia* (London: Penguin, 1996). See also Warren Zimmermann, *Origins of a Catastrophe* (New York: Times Books, 1996). Zimmermann was the last US Ambassador to Federal Yugoslavia.

17 The ICRC was in touch with, and consulted by, the major Western political figures in this conflict. See for example, David Owen, *Balkan Odyssey* (New York: Harcourt Brace, 1995).

18 See further Forsythe, *The Humanitarians*, 108–15.

19 Ignatieff, *The Warrior's Honor*.

20 See in this regard Larry Minear, Jeffrey Clark, Roberta Cohen, Dennis Gallagher, Iain Guest and Thomas G. Weiss, "Humanitarian Action in the Former Yugoslavia," Brown University, Watson Institute, Paper #18, 1994.

21 See further in particular Sadako Ogata, *The Turbulent Decade: Confronting the Refugee Crises of the 1990s* (New York: Norton, 2005), 50–171.

22 See the book review by Mark Danner in the *New York Review of Books* at www.markdanner.com/articles/62/print.

23 See further Samantha Power, *A Problem from Hell: America and the Age of Genocide* (New York: Perennial, 2002).

24 The ICTY, in the Krstic case, found a certain Serb commander guilty of genocide for his role in the massacre at Srebrenica, in which a large number of Bosnian Muslim men and boys of fighting age were intentionally killed in 1995 while under the control of Serbs. Whether this was a proper interpretation of the UN Genocide Convention of 1948, which prohibits the intention to destroy, in whole or in part, an ethnic, national, racial, or religious group, is an interesting question. There are other court cases pertaining to genocide in the western Balkans in the 1990s.

25 See further Richard Holbrooke, *To End a War* (New York: Random House, 1998).

26 Michele Mercier, *Crimes Sans Châtiment* (Brussels, Belgium: Bruylant, 1994).

27 For good overviews see the appropriate chapters in Lori Fisler Damrosch, ed., *Enforcing Restraint* (New York: Council on Foreign Relations Press, 1993); and James Mayall, ed., *The New Interventionism 1991–1994* (Cambridge: Cambridge University Press, 1996).

28 Forsythe, *The Humanitarians*, 117.

29 See the popular rendition in Mark Bowden, *Blackhawk Down* (New York: Atlantic Monthly Press, 1999), which was made into a movie.

30 See further ICRC Annual Report, 2004, 98–101.

31 See further ICRC Annual Report, 2004, 98–101.

32 See further Mohamed Sahnoun, *Somalia: The Missed Opportunities* (Washington, DC: USIP Press, 1994). In this work an Algerian diplomat, who held positions at the UN and was deeply involved in the diplomacy for

Somalia in the early 1990s, compares the ICRC favorably to various other organizations.

33 Jean-Francois Fayet and Peter Huber, "La Mission Wehrlin du CICR en Union Sovietique (1920–1938)," *International Review of the Red Cross*, vol. 85, no. 849 (2003): 95–117, at 105.

34 www.icrc.org/Web/Eng/siteeng0.nsf/iwpList410/AAC4E916402377B FC125 6B66005F18Ee.

35 ICRC, "Armed Conflict and Family Links," www.icrc.org.web/eng/siteeng. nsf/iwpList410/21904DDE2BEA0D77C1256C5B002D991B.

5   Detention visits

- **Detention visits: some history and law**
- **Detention visits: ICRC basic policies**
- **Detention visits: the US war on terrorism**
- **Conclusion**

Within many legal and military circles, the ICRC is reasonably well known as the agency that conducts visits to prisoners of war (POWs) in international armed conflict. In 2004, at a time of increased attention within the United States to the treatment of "enemy prisoners," James Schlesinger, former US secretary of defense, referred to the ICRC in rather demeaning terms as an organization that "is essentially an auditing function for detainees."[1] The organization visits more prisoners around the world, in various legal categories, than any other agency.

In this chapter we begin with some historical and legal background on ICRC prison visits and then offer an overview of ICRC policy for detainees. Next we provide a short case study of the ICRC, prisoners, and the US "war against terrorism."

Detention visits: some history and law

As noted in our second chapter on the history of the ICRC, the organization first became involved with conducting prison visits during World War I. While assisting wounded soldiers in the POW camps, the ICRC found a more general humanitarian need. Detained combatants who were not wounded were also in need of proper nourishment and humane treatment. So as a practical matter, and without any authorization from the existing Geneva Convention of 1906, the ICRC began broadscale POW visits.[2] It exercised its right of initiative to undertake new humanitarian tasks, by seeking and securing the consent of the relevant states.

ICRC prison visits to POWs during this era did not entail the principle of discretion. ICRC reports were public documents, often sold. ICRC practical experience with POW visits led to the 1929 Geneva Convention for Prisoners of War. Even then, the details of ICRC visits were not spelled out in that Convention, but rather left to ICRC practice. Nothing was said in the 1929 law, for example, about the obligation of states to allow ICRC visits, or about publicity and discretion, or about the disposition of reports. All of this was left to the ICRC.

Even in 1949, when the third GC was negotiated for protection of POWs, the details of ICRC visits were left to practice. Again in 1977, when Additional Protocol I was added to the 1949 GCs dealing with international armed conflict, the written law was silent on the details of ICRC visits. From 1949, in international armed conflict, ICRC visits to both POWs and civilian detainees became obligatory. However, such visits could be delayed for (exceptional) military necessity, if the dangers of hostilities prevented them.[3]

Especially important for prisoner matters is Additional Protocol I, Article 75. It indicates that in international war, if prisoners are not considered either POWs under the Third 1949 GC, or civilian detainees under the Fourth 1949 GC, they are still entitled to certain minimum standards of humane treatment. Explicitly prohibited is "torture of all kinds, whether physical or mental," and "outrages upon personal dignity, in particular humiliating and degrading treatment," as well as "threats to commit any of the foregoing acts."

The same ethical thinking that broadened the ICRC's active concern from wounded soldiers to other combatants *hors de combat* in international war carried the organization into the realm of security prisoners, sometimes called political prisoners. We have already noted how, in the immediate aftermath of World War I, the ICRC started visiting prisoners in places like Hungary and Russia, even though those states did not see themselves as officially still at war. The fact that governments might refer to the situation as one of domestic unrest or instability did not cause the ICRC to back off. What was compelling for the organization was that the government tended to view certain prisoners as enemies. For the ICRC, this view placed the prisoner in danger of abuse. Hence the organization considered these prisoners in need of neutral humanitarian protection. And so began the ICRC's work with security or political prisoners, which became more and more systematic over time. Whereas other organizations, like Amnesty International, founded in 1961, were often associated in the public's mind with "political prisoners," it was in fact the ICRC that was seeking to protect at least some of them (those related to violent political conflict) beginning around 1919–1920.

To complicate matters still further, increasingly the notion took hold that there could be an internal war rather than an international war.[4] In such violent situations there were, of course, prisoners taken. In law, when such prisoners are also combatants, they are not called prisoners of war. In addition, when such prisoners are civilians, they are not called civilian detainees. The law is controlled by states and their governments, as we saw in Chapter 4. States are reluctant to include challenges to the domestic status quo as on a par with international war. In particular, governments do not want to give fighters in civil wars, when captured, the "exalted status" of "prisoner of war." So as far as legal wording is concerned, state interest in image and status trumps humanitarian concern. Nevertheless, by whatever name, the ICRC became systematically concerned with prisoners in internal or civil wars. After all, if the agency was concerned with prisoners in international war and in situations of domestic troubles and tensions, why not be concerned about prisoners in civil wars?

So, in cases like the (internationalized) Spanish Civil War in the 1930s, the ICRC was active on prisoner matters.[5] ICRC experience in the Spanish Civil War and other places contributed to Common Article 3 in the 1949 GCs. This one article, common to the four treaties of 1949, constitutes the first written provision in international law on civil wars. It provides, among other things, that prisoners are to be treated humanely, and when tried for crimes are entitled to minimum standards of due process.

The details for Common Article 3 are spelled out in Box 3.1. The agreed content, in turn, led to 1977 Additional Protocol II.[6] For the ICRC and for most persons interested in the practical application of IHL, the central point is this regarding prisoners: prisoners in civil wars are entitled to certain minimal humanitarian protections, even though they may not be called prisoners of war or civilian detainees by governments. The 1949 Common Article 3 provides for this protection in general language. The 1977 Additional Protocol II spells out these protections in more detail.

To summarize with a view to practical prisoner protection and ICRC policy:

1   the view of the nature of the conflict affects legal obligation;
2   state legal obligation to protect POWs and civilian detainees is most developed and most demanding in international wars, where the Third and Fourth 1949 GCs, and 1977 AP I, provide detailed rules, including ICRC obligatory visits;

3   states have legal obligations to protect prisoners in internal wars, where 1949 GC Common Article 3 and 1977 AP II provide fewer detailed guidelines and where ICRC visits are not obligatory; and
4   in violence falling short of armed conflict, these domestic troubles and tensions are not covered by any IHL, but rather by human rights law (for example, the UN Convention Against Torture, prohibiting torture and mistreatment) and by the ICRC's unspecified right of initiative.[7]

Detention visits: ICRC basic policies

The history and legal considerations noted above do affect ICRC efforts for the humanitarian protection of prisoners, but particularly the legal complexities can obscure a certain common approach by the organization, regardless of legal categories. The ICRC has devised a set procedure for the actual visit, regardless of the legal type of conflict or legal status of prisoners. It consists of an initial interview with prison authorities, then a visit without witnesses with the prisoners themselves, or in certain cases a spokesperson for large numbers of prisoners, and then a concluding interview with prison authorities in which basic findings are presented in verbal form.[8] Later a formal report is submitted.[9] Follow-up visits are scheduled to ascertain the progress made in correcting any reported problems. In certain exceptional cases, a visit might occur even if private, confidential talks with prisoners cannot be arranged at first, for example to demonstrate an initial process to a skeptical detaining authority. But prisoner discussions in the presence of the detaining authority are to be avoided in principle.

It is not clear to an outsider how the ICRC controls for electronic eavesdropping by modern detaining authorities. Certainly many states have the capacity to "listen in" at considerable distance without a representative being present when the ICRC delegate talks to a prisoner. This being the case, some detainees have been punished for what they said to the ICRC, and some prisoners have stopped talking to the ICRC. Naturally the organization can protest to the controlling authorities when this happens. The ICRC reserves the right to make its continued discretion conditional on adequate humanitarian progress. But a close reading of many detention situations leaves some unanswered questions about confidential interviews and the integrity of ICRC policies and practices.

Regarding detention visits, the focus is on the conditions of detention and not the reasons for detention. That is to say, the ICRC does not pass judgment on the legality or the legitimacy of the reasons for detention. However, sometimes the ICRC will seek release because of a prisoner's health or other humanitarian consideration.

The ICRC has a very clear policy on how to treat the situations it finds during its visits.[10] The organization believes in a discreet approach in which problems are addressed in quiet diplomacy with the detaining authority. This is viewed as especially helpful for access and impact in situations of internal wars and domestic troubles and tensions where the ICRC has no right of obligatory or automatic visit under IHL. One has to ask for access, and the promise of quiet diplomacy is seen as advantageous to obtaining access. At this point discussions are bilateral between the ICRC and the detaining authority. The ICRC first seeks cooperation without public fanfare.

The ICRC believes detaining authorities should be given a certain but unspecified time to correct problems in humanitarian conditions. The ICRC is looking for a good faith effort by the prison authorities to respond to ICRC concerns, based as they are on standards in IHL, or human rights law. A key feature to this process is the agreement by the authorities to allow repeated visits without witnesses.

One can, in fact, tell something about the process from the outside. If visits occur every six months or yearly, then the situation is not likely to be too terrible. If, on the other hand, Geneva announces that visits are occurring every two weeks, then it is reasonable to conclude that there are pressing problems.

Should there not be significant improvement over time, the ICRC reserves the right to involve third parties in the process, in a confidential effort to achieve the desired humanitarian progress. Thus, when dealing with certain states or other armed actors known to have close friends or allies, the ICRC may contact these third parties. For example, in the past when dealing with the Iraqi government of Saddam Hussein, the ICRC sought to make progress on certain humanitarian issues by involving the Palestine Liberation Organization (PLO) in certain discussions. Given long standing problems in the prisons of India holding suspected militants related to Kashmir, the ICRC took up some issues with the United States (a fact which leaked to social media and complicated Indian–ICRC relations).

As a last resort, the ICRC reserves the right to make a public denunciation of egregious violations of IHL or human rights standards, when there has not been acceptable progress on these matters over time, and if the organization judges that such a public denunciation would aid the prisoners being victimized. In general it can be said that the ICRC does not very much like to take this step, does not in general believe in the effectiveness of public protests, and believes that the frequent use of such public denunciations will harm its access to other prisoners in other situations. One is hard pressed to find many examples of such a public criticism when the ICRC is dealing with a major state.

Contributing to the ICRC's hesitancy about public criticism is the fact that often the ICRC is the prisoners' only contact with the outside world, which is very important for the mental health of the prisoners. Lech Walesa, leader of the Solidarity movement during the latter stages of the communist era in Poland, and a prisoner visited by the ICRC, has said the following:

> For most people deprived of their freedom, the most important issue is not their political fight, but often their sheer survival, their humane treatment and the preservation of one's dignity. [ICRC] visits gave reassurance to detainees that they were not forgotten and that there was still hope. It is extremely valuable for every person to know that. … [T]he detainees who are visited know that they are not forgotten, they are less afraid, and their families are reassured. These are very important issues.[11]

Sometimes the ICRC may ask prisoners if the organization should continue with visits, even without much progress in conditions, or suspend visits with a public announcement. If the prisoners want a continuation of visits, how can the ICRC do otherwise, given the importance of those visits for a prisoner's mental health? The ICRC asked Nelson Mandela, when he was imprisoned in South Africa during the apartheid era, if the organization should stop visits because of lack of important progress in improving detention conditions. He told the ICRC representative to continue with visits, otherwise the ICRC would not be in a position to stop the bad that might occur in the future.[12]

On the other hand, the ICRC is aware that if it is present in the face of major and repeated prisoner abuse and says nothing, it will be seen as an accomplice to evil, which will damage its reputation and role. It knows that its presence in a country may be used by the detaining authority for its own purposes ("the ICRC is here, so the situation cannot be bad") and thus the organization tries to satisfy itself that prisoner conditions over time do actually justify its continued presence in-country.[13]

It is possible that there is a slight tendency toward bolder public statements regarding prisoner matters. A striking example occurred in 2006, when the organization publicly noted that it had felt compelled to suspend prison visits in Chechnya due to lack of cooperation from

Russia, and that ICRC President Kellenberger was prepared to meet with Russian President Vladimir Putin to resolve matters.[14] This seemed an obvious effort to generate public pressure on the highest levels of the Russian state. At the time of writing it was difficult to document the results of this process.

If authorities release selected or distorted information about prisoner conditions, the ICRC reserves the right to release entire reports or otherwise correct distortions. The organization will serve as a conduit to convey complaints about prisoners from third parties, but the ICRC itself tries to avoid passing public judgment on such controversies.

It refuses to allow its personnel to testify in criminal court cases regarding what has been seen in detention centers, believing that such judicial testimony would adversely affect its access and thus impact on conditions. This policy has been accepted by the UN's ad hoc criminal courts (for former Yugoslavia, and Rwanda), and by the International Criminal Court. In the old terminology of the organization, it preferred charity to justice. It still sees its primary role as pragmatically advancing humanitarian protection on the ground, leaving to others a more punitive legal justice. This is an interesting, paradoxical position for the "guardian of IHL," an organization that has lots of lawyers and helps develop IHL. But the criminal application of IHL is normally left to others. Public denunciation of war crimes would be a last resort, when all hope was lost about securing any cooperation from the authority in question. Even in dealing with Saddam Hussein's government in 1991, when the ICRC was blocked from POW visits and not allowed into occupied Kuwait, the ICRC still did not publicly denounce those policies that violated IHL until that war was virtually over.

Likewise after 11 September 2001, US authorities in the George W. Bush Administration engaged in the forced disappearance and abuse of prisoners held by the CIA in secret prisons. The ICRC was barred. In US military prisons, especially during 2002–2005, certain prisoners were hidden from the ICRC, supposedly private interviews were monitored, and a certain number of prisoners were seriously abused. The ICRC publically denounced these CIA "black sites". Being present in most military prisons, at least after a certain time, the ICRC made public comments about the mental health of prisoners adversely affected by having no clear legal framework for their detention and thus no clear idea about prospective release. Its other concerns were treated with its customary discretion. At one point it did quietly suspend its visits to the Abu Ghraib prison in Iraq in 2004 to protest the atrocious conditions there. Several ICRC reports about US military prisons leaked to the public, but there is no evidence that the ICRC was responsible. Indeed,

أ di ffering interps. of IHL

the ICRC protested the leaks, fearing this would complicate its access to other prisoners.

This approach to detention visits can allow for some undesired problems to develop. For example, if I am a prison official for a repressive state and have illiberal values, and I know the ICRC, I may very well offer a little cooperation and progress here and there, while continuing with some major violations of human dignity. Knowing that the ICRC is a conservative, patient, Swiss organization (at least at the top), I can count on it to prefer quiet diplomacy, to want to avoid public judgments or denunciations, and to justify its low-key role as long as some progress can be shown. After all, if it pulls out in protest, it is out of the humanitarian game and on the sidelines with Amnesty International, Human Rights Watch, and other human rights advocacy groups. A denunciation and withdrawal costs the ICRC its special, inside role on the ground.

So if I want to torture certain prisoners, I give the ICRC access to other prisoners. If I want to maintain secret detention sites hidden from the organization, I give them access to other detention facilities where less important prisoners are held. And maybe while this game of cat and mouse is going on, I am able to get the information I want through torture, or even perhaps kill off those most dangerous to my position. Pinochet basically did this in Chile after 1973, cooperating with the ICRC with regard to certain prisoner matters, but killing some 6,000 perceived leftist subversives during that time, and torturing still others who were hidden from the organization.

This scenario is not all that different in its general outlines from ICRC interaction with the United States after the terrorist attacks of 11 September 2001.

Detention visits: the US war on terrorism

While some, even some within the ICRC, may see that organization as the high priest of humanitarianism, the fact is that IHL, like IL in general, is often interpreted in a decentralized process. The ICRC may be entitled to its view of the meaning of IHL, but states do not have to defer to its view. As long as differing legal opinions do not get adjudicated in an international court, or resolved in a legally binding decision of the UN Security Council, which is what frequently occurs, states—as a practical or policy matter—are left with the freedom to make their own (self-serving) interpretations. This is so unless domestic courts take up the question of the laws of war, which most domestic courts are reluctant to do, since it may involve challenging the executive over matters of national security.

For example, the ICRC and most states have taken the position that Israeli control of territory taken during and after the 1967 war is regulated by IHL. Israel, however, has maintained the position that because much of this territory was not part of another state in 1967, it is therefore not occupied territory in the sense of the Fourth 1949 GC. The lack of authoritative international court judgment, combined with the lack of effective enforcement, has allowed Israel to maintain its distinctly minority position on this legal question.

When looking at the US "war on terrorism" which developed in the aftermath of 11 September 2001, we see that the ICRC has run into difficulties in trying to implement its view of IHL. Executive branch interpretations have been key, as well as a few national court cases.

The first question that concerns us here is whether what the United States calls "the war on terrorism" is an armed conflict in the legal sense of the term. Did the 9/11 attacks by Al Qaeda commence a war under the general understanding of the term? If so, then the Geneva Conventions should apply and countries such as the United States and Great Britain, among others participating in the global campaign, states that are parties to the Geneva Conventions, have legal obligations under the treaties. The second question is, what was the actual treatment of enemy prisoners, and what role did the ICRC play?

Afghanistan and Gitmo: detention

The United States gained control over Guantanamo Bay, Cuba, as a result of the Spanish-American War of 1889. During this short war, the Spanish lost their colonial possession, Cuba, as a result of US military victory. In return, the United States leased Guantanamo Bay from the Cuban authorities forever (in perpetuity). Guantanamo Bay, or Gitmo as it is sometimes called, has been a US military base for decades.

The ICRC has argued that individuals picked up in Afghanistan in the winter of 2001–2002 and who may not be covered by certain provisions of the Geneva Conventions nevertheless are entitled to protection under international law:

> Persons not covered by either the Third or the Fourth Geneva Convention in international armed conflict are entitled to the fundamental guarantees provided for by customary international law (as reflected in Article 75 of Additional Protocol I), as well as by applicable domestic and human rights law. All these legal sources provide for rights of detainees in relation to treatment, conditions and due process of law.[15]

It is very clear that the Bush Administration disagreed with this view and sought to erase any legal framework that would interfere with tough interrogation of suspected terrorists in the immediate aftermath of the 9/11 attacks.[16] Bush Administration officials especially wanted to place prisoners at Guantanamo in a legal black hole. It is the Justice Department that is officially responsible for making determinations of US obligations under international law. In the fall of 2001, a tough bureaucratic battle ensued in the administration over the relevance of IHL and also the UN Convention Against Torture. The victors in this struggle were principally US Vice President Cheney, and some individuals in the Justice and Defense departments. The result was a series of pronouncements by the Justice Department, with Deputy Assistant Attorney General John Yoo as chief memo writer, which were then accepted by the White House, first by the president's lawyer at that time, Alberto Gonzales (later attorney general), and President Bush himself.

The first thrust of these memos and public statements was to eliminate all of IHL as a relevant legal factor in the ensuing violence and capture of persons in Afghanistan.[17] The administration's argument was that the US fight in Afghanistan was with Al Qaeda, a non-state actor that was not a party to IHL and did not follow IHL rules. For example, Yoo argued in a memo of 9 January 2002 that the Geneva Conventions dealt with armed conflict between states (Article 2) and a civil war within a nation-state (Article 3 and Protocol II) but not with transnational terrorism. Therefore, the Geneva Conventions do not apply to any of the detainees from the violence in Afghanistan. This view was initially endorsed by the Bush Administration, in memos for example by the attorney general, Alberto Gonzales.

Furthermore, Bush officials argued that the Geneva Conventions are dated and do not conform to the reality of the twenty-first century. In a 25 January 2002 memorandum for the president, Alberto Gonzalez specifically argued that the third Geneva Convention on the Treatment of Prisoners of War was outdated.

The nature of the new war places a high premium on other factors, such as the ability to quickly obtain information from captured terrorists and their sponsors in order to avoid further atrocities against American civilians, and the need to try terrorists for war crimes such as wantonly killing civilians. In my judgment, this new paradigm renders obsolete Geneva's strict limitations on questioning of enemy prisoners and renders quaint some of its provisions.[18]

The president himself declared that no detainees at the US military facility at Gitmo were protected persons within the meaning of IHL. This view was then communicated to those serving at Gitmo. One soldier noted in an account of his time at Gitmo that Captain Henderson (JAG) specifically told the military personnel that the third and fourth GCs did not apply to the more than 600 individuals at Gitmo who were suspected of having Al Qaeda ties.[19]

This argument is peculiar, to put it mildly, because the application of IHL, particularly the 1949 GCs, does not depend on the nature of various factions, but on whether a state is the locus of hostilities with an outside power (international war) or internal armed group (internal war).[20] According to the usual understanding of IHL, which was articulated by the ICRC,[21] when the United States used its air force to bomb targets in Afghanistan starting in the fall of 2001, and sent in its military forces both to direct that bombing and to participate in various ways in hostilities on the ground, an international war existed to which the bulk of IHL applied. This traditional view was adopted by the United Kingdom, for example.

Now it may be the case, factually speaking, that in addition to international war Afghanistan was also characterized in late 2001 and early 2002 by an internal war between the Taliban and the Northern Alliance. In any event, either the IHL for internal war applied, or the IHL for international war applied, or both. It defies traditional understanding to claim that no IHL applied to the extensive international and internal violence occurring in Afghanistan during late 2001 and early 2002. This means that persons captured in the context of that violence were either POWs in the meaning of the Third 1949 GC, or civilian detainees in the meaning of the Fourth 1949 GC, or protected persons in the meaning of 1949 Common Article 3. It was not legally well considered for the US administration to say that no person detained as a result of those hostilities, and especially no person transferred from Afghanistan to the US detention facility at Guantanamo Bay, Cuba, fell under IHL.[22]

It was significant that Bush administration pronouncements about IHL were opposed by a number of former US military officials, who feared that playing fast and loose with IHL would endanger US military personnel in the future.[23] Secretary of State Colin Powell encouraged the president to apply the GCs to the conflict in Afghanistan because upholding the GC would present "a positive international posture, preserve US credibility and moral authority by taking the high ground, and put us in a better position to demand and receive international support."[24] Furthermore, he suggested that "the U.S. has never determined that GPW (Geneva Prisoners of War Convention) did not apply to an armed conflict in which its forces have been engaged ... the GPW was intended to cover all types of armed conflict and did not by its terms limit its application."[25]

The second thrust of administration pronouncements was to minimize any relevance of the UN Convention Against Torture, which prohibits at all times and in all places not only the torture of persons but also treatment that is cruel, degrading, or humiliating. So Yoo and others tried to say that unless US officials intended to inflict severe pain, or unless organ failure occurred, the treaty did not come into play. These "interpretations" were so bizarre that they were eventually retracted when publicized. They did, however, as a practical matter, give legal cover to those US personnel who might be charged with violation of law. Such persons could say: "but executive memos said it was alright to do this or that." The effect of various memos by US civilian lawyers in the Bush Administration was to give a "get out of jail card" to those who might be charged with crimes under international law—at least in US courts.

At the same time, from early 2002, the administration allowed the ICRC to maintain a permanent presence at Gitmo and to evaluate the conditions of detention there apart from any formal acceptance of IHL. The contradiction between the US tough approach to interrogation at Gitmo, so clear in retrospect, and allowing an ICRC presence is not yet fully explained. One view is that, while some cooperation with the ICRC was decided on in December 2001 or January 2002 by lower-level military officials, it was not until mid-2002 that US Secretary of Defense Donald Rumsfeld wanted more actionable intelligence from the prisoners at Gitmo, and hence dispatched General Geoffrey Miller to toughen interrogation procedures.[26]

In any event, with regard to Gitmo, the ICRC pressed US authorities, sometimes in testy exchanges, to change certain practices.

In early 2002, the Bush administration began sending individuals captured in Afghanistan and elsewhere and suspected of having ties to Al Qaeda to Gitmo. Various techniques were employed during interrogations of at least some of these individuals to obtain actionable intelligence.[27] Some detainees were sexually abused (having their genitals grabbed by a female interrogator), others were religiously provoked (one female interrogator smeared fake menstrual blood on a detainee to make the individual feel impure). In general at Gitmo, for a time US authorities used "torture lite" in the form of sleep deprivation, extremes of heat and cold, subjection to loud music, and other techniques to break prisoners' will and extract information. Military dogs were sometimes used to terrify prisoners. One of the biggest problems was the fact of indefinite detention without much prospect of charge or trial, and the ICRC made a public, if low-key, protest over this as early as May 2003.

Many, perhaps 15 to 20 percent of the total detained in the 2002–2005 period, were physically abused. One soldier stationed at Gitmo described the abuse:

> Getting IRFed at (Camp)X-ray meant receiving a good old-fashioned ass whipping, after which the unlucky detainee would be hogtied, made to kneel with his hands behind his back and his hand and foot shackles locked together for 4 hours.[28]

In June 2006, three Gitmo prisoners committed suicide, which renewed focus on that issue.

There have been numerous criticisms leveled at the conditions at Gitmo. Amnesty International, Human Rights Watch, Human Rights First, the Center for Constitutional Rights (NY), and the American Civil Liberties Union have all complained about the treatments of detainees and the lack of legal protections and indefinite detention. Of particular concern was the excessive use of force, chaining and shackling of prisoners, leaving prisoners naked for extended periods of time, abuse of medical ethics, and the lack of a proper trial or judicial hearing for the detainees at Gitmo.[29]

The ICRC has criticized the conditions at Gitmo, saying in a confidential report to the US government that the physical and psychological coercion used on detainees was "tantamount to torture." In addition, the ICRC, in a confidential report in July 2004, criticized the medical practices of Gitmo, saying that detainees' medical reports were not private or confidential but used by interrogators to gain information. Concerns were raised about the use of loud noise, solitary confinement for long periods of time, sexual humiliation, and beatings. Various reports from Gitmo document that there have been numerous suicide attempts.[30] In an ICRC press release of 16 January 2004, President Kellenberger "lamented the fact that two years after the first detainees arrived at Gitmo, and despite repeated pleas, they are still facing indefinite detention beyond the reach of the law."[31] Some individuals detained at Gitmo were later released after the US government determined they were innocent. For example, Gul Zaman was released in April 2005 after spending three and a half years at Gitmo.[32] But this occurred after those individuals had been in legal limbo for years.

Over time there was a certain improvement in Gitmo's conditions, according to ICRC President Kellenberger in a press conference in

2005. But in keeping with policies on discretion, he did not say exactly what practices had ceased and what the remaining problems were.[33] There have also been reports of torture and deaths in Afghanistan.

In December 2002, in a Bagram prison 40 miles north of the capital, Kabul, two Afghans were killed (Dilawar, Mullah Habibullah). The deaths of these prisoners were a result of physical assaults by American military personnel. Each man had been left in his cell, shackled by the wrists to the ceiling. The shackling of detainees was used to cause pain and deprive them of sleep. Both men had been beaten and kicked repeatedly.[34] Specialist Brand admitted that he struck Dilawar over thirty times. Army medical examiners concluded that both suffered "blunt-force injuries" to their legs.[35]

At the same time that ICRC visits were occurring at Gitmo and in various places in Afghanistan, with some improvement in conditions, the United States held other prisoners in secret locales, or "black sites," to which the ICRC was given no access. Here we see the pattern noted in Chile and elsewhere, in which a detaining authority will provide some cooperation with the ICRC on selected issues, but not on others. Whatever the humanitarian progress at Gitmo and in Afghanistan in military facilities, President Kellenberger in the spring of 2006 "deplored" the fact that the ICRC had no access to certain US prisoners related to its "war" on terrorism.[36] There did not appear to be any reaction in the United States to this exceptionally strong public language by the ICRC.

Also, the United States (and certain other states) continued with "rendition," which was little more than a policy of state kidnapping and secret extra-legal deportation. Persons would be seized wherever, and then secretly sent to friendly states where they would be interrogated, presumably free from any supervision by US courts. Some of these persons might or might not be eventually placed in Gitmo. It was obvious why someone might be seized and then sent to places like Egypt or Uzbekistan, since the US State Department's own annual human rights reports indicated that torture was prevalent in these states. The UN Convention Against Torture prohibits states from engaging in such a practice. Some states, Great Britain for example, when transferring a prisoner to Jordan, indicated they insisted on assurances of proper treatment. The value of such diplomatic niceties was open to question. So overall, with regard to Afghanistan and Gitmo, the Bush Administration in its "war on terrorism" engaged in policies of disappeared persons and torture lite (and in Afghanistan sometimes torture heavy, with fatalities as proof). At the same time, particularly at Gitmo, one could surmise some improvement over time.

The ICRC would occasionally make certain public criticisms (about mental health problems from indefinite detention without trial, or about lack of access to persons held in secret locales). The record known thus far suggests that the ICRC pressed hard for changes, especially at Gitmo, but overall its relationship with administration authorities was reasonably good and stable by 2006. Whether it should have spoken out more about Gitmo and Afghanistan can only be finally determined at a future point when more information is known.

Iraq: detention

When in March 2003 the United States invaded Iraq, removed the government of Saddam Hussein (and eventually captured him), and then tried to control the country, Washington agreed that this was an international armed conflict followed by occupation. Therefore, the 1949 GCs applied, under which the ICRC was entitled to visit detainees against the background of the detailed provisions of, especially, the Third and Fourth GCs. After the ICRC's headquarters in Baghdad were attacked in October of 2003, the ICRC set up shop in Jordan and brought its expatriate (non-Iraqi) personnel into the country for detention visits.

From late summer 2003 into the fall, the ICRC became aware of major violations of human dignity in Abu Ghraib and other prisons in Iraq run by the United States. Abu Ghraib was a prison with a notorious reputation for inhumane treatment under the regime of Saddam Hussein. After major hostilities ended in 2003, the US military took control of the prison. At times ICRC delegates quietly suspended visits in protest against conditions. They submitted the usual candid reports to US authorities.

In early 2004, American pictures of abuse began to circulate in private circles. These photos were reproduced in the American media, creating a major brouhaha in Washington and the country. The pictures also caused a significant backlash against the Bush administration in world public opinion, especially in the Arab-Islamic world. These major violations of IHL, and of human decency, proved a bonanza for Al Qaeda and its allies. Some participants in the growing insurgency in Iraq against the US presence were carrying pictures of the abuse at Abu Ghraib when they were apprehended. Failure of the United States to treat prisoners in accordance with IHL proved a major obstacle to its efforts to win the hearts and minds of people in Iraq, and especially in the Arab-Islamic world.

The domestic and international condemnations of the abuses at Abu Ghraib led to a number of investigations. Some (the Schlesinger

Report) suggested that the abuse of prisoners at Abu Ghraib was the work of a few isolated individuals or "bad apples." The executive summary of the Church Report found no evidence to suggest that the Pentagon or White House pressured those on the ground to abuse or torture detainees at Abu Ghraib in an effort to obtain information.[37] US authorities moved to court martial or otherwise sanction a number of lower-ranking military persons for their involvement in prisoner mistreatment in Iraq. Higher officers, however, responsible for the training and supervision of these rank-and-file persons were not sanctioned, generally speaking. One reservist brigadier general and one active duty colonel were punished. However, Ricardo Sanchez, the overall commander of US forces in Iraq, who at one point had authorized coercive interrogation techniques, and who allowed a confusing and unclear situation to develop, was never legally sanctioned. He was, however, denied promotion and effectively forced into retirement. Also escaping attention was General Geoffrey Miller, who had been commander at Gitmo, and who was transferred to Iraq by the office of the Secretary of Defense to institute the same kinds of interrogation techniques in Iraq that had been employed at Gitmo. Thus military and civilian leaders who authorized the interrogation techniques that resulted in violations of IHL have not been held accountable.[38]

There have also been allegations of wrong-doing in other parts of Iraq. The ACLU has released documents implicating army commanders with interfering with investigations concerning the death of detainees in Tikrit and Mosul. Furthermore, the *New York Times* reported that a former Iraqi general, Major General Abed Hamed Mowhoush, was suffocated when an army interrogator put a sleeping bag over his head. The army interrogator was found guilty of negligent homicide, but let off on the more serious charge of murder.[39]

A leaked ICRC report argued that the abuse was not the result of a few individuals. It said that ICRC delegates observed prisoner abuse that was systematic, not isolated, and based on an interrogation policy which demanded actionable intelligence.[40] Furthermore, it has been suggested that the CIA kept approximately 30 "ghost detainees" at Abu Ghraib in an effort to prevent the ICRC from gaining access to them.

The ICRC never made a public protest about Abu Ghraib and other US detention facilities in Iraq, although a public protest was debated within the organization and desired by delegates on the scene. ICRC press releases of the era were more about Gitmo and Afghanistan than about Iraq. It does seem to be the case that it was the private photos, and not ICRC confidential reports, that brought about major attention to the problems from early 2004.[41] Its candid reports about Abu Ghraib had simply been dismissed by US military and other authorities.

While some of the abuse at Abu Ghraib appears to have been unauthorized, it occurred in a context in which the abuse of certain prisoners in certain places *had* been authorized, and in which the Bush Administration had played fast and loose with interpretations of IHL. It was in this sense that the 2001 memos in Washington, gutting the 1949 Geneva Conventions and UN torture convention, proved to be the start of the road that led to Abu Ghraib. The usual military guidelines about detention and interrogation had been said not to apply, but exactly what rules did apply was not fully clear.

Just as Secretary of Defense Rumsfeld had demanded more actionable intelligence out of Gitmo midway through 2002, so US officials sought more actionable intelligence in Iraq as the anti-American insurgency mounted from May 2003. Certain prisoners in Iraq were hidden from the ICRC, by conscious US policy, in an effort to gain information. It was in this context that the Abu Ghraib abuse occurred. Therefore, unauthorized actions by lower-ranking personnel need to be seen in the larger context of the decisions by high officials, civilian and military, to minimize, if not eliminate, legal and organizational protections for prisoners taken in violent conflict. Once one authorizes coercive interrogation for some, it becomes difficult to implement humane interrogation for others.

Immediately after 9/11, the United States was the beneficiary of much sympathy in the world, as shown by public opinion polls. Governments supported US initiatives in the UN Security Council, and citizens in many countries stood in line to sign a condolence book in US embassies and consulates. This broad goodwill was dissipated by the Bush Administration in 2002 and 2003, and thereafter, in two major ways: (1) its policy toward enemy detainees; and (2) the Bush doctrine of unilateral preventative war, particularly as implemented in Iraq. Polls showed a precipitous drop in foreign support for US policies, even in normally friendly states like Turkey, Jordan, and Indonesia. In some European countries, China was more respected than the United States.

The ICRC, operating in a context characterized by much American ultra-nationalism and unilateralism, had persistently stuck to its views about the relevance of IHL in much of the US "war on terrorism." This position found at least some vindication in a US Supreme Court ruling of June 2006.[42] Perhaps more importantly, it had stuck to its usual policies of seeking discrete cooperation on the ground over time, while making a few public comments. It both criticized certain US policies (indefinite detention at Gitmo without legal charge or trial;

hiding prisoners in "black sites"), and indicated some progress in humanitarian matters at Gitmo.[43]

Case summary

From the vantage point of 2015, it seems fairly clear that during the period from 2002 to about 2005–2006, the Bush Administration was determined to use abusive interrogations to try to gain actionable intelligence to prevent further terrorist attacks on the US homeland and installations abroad. US policy seemed similar to British and Israeli policy in other conflicts in that coercive interrogation was employed but with an intention to avoid certain techniques (e.g., pulling out fingernails) and above all the death of the prisoner. During this era the ICRC seemed largely unable to stop or mitigate prisoner abuse in the military detention centers where it had access. (It was barred from CIA secret prisons until they were presumably closed in 2006.) The ICRC was thoughtful and diligent in its efforts, but most of the abuse was authorized and monitored and not the result of "bad apples."

To the extent that US detention conditions improved over time, it seems that this occurred because of a push back against Bush policies within the United States. In 2005 the Congress passed the Detainee Treatment Act which reaffirmed that US military prisons were required to use humane interrogation techniques. This congressional action came after unauthorized photos of prisoner abuse at the Abu Ghraib prison in Iraq surfaced in social media and shocked the nation. Many of the actions going on at Abu Ghraib were similar to authorized measures already implemented at Gitmo and the CIA Black Sites. Also, in 2006, the US Supreme Court held that all persons held at Gitmo were protected at least by GC Common Article 3. This 1949 provision of IHL prohibited inhumane acts against a variety of persons in internal armed conflict. The Supreme Court held that these protections should obtain in all armed conflicts as a base line standard.

The Barack Obama administration sought to close the books on US torture and cruel treatment of enemy detainees and attempted to close Gitmo prison, although that administration did not seek legal punishment for those who had authorized the previous abuse. At the time of writing Congress had blocked the closure of Gitmo, passing legislation that prevented the Obama team from transferring remaining detainees there to mainland prisons. There also continued to be controversy over the use of military commissions to try certain presumed enemy prisoners for war crimes such as attacking civilians. The Obama team

only actor capable...

preferred to use federal courts rather than military commissions, the latter being controversial, slow, and entangled in various procedural disputes. By 2015 few detainees had been convicted in the Commissions, whereas it was clear that federal courts were capable of trying terror suspects while protecting sensitive sources and information.

As a political fact, Republicans tended to support abusive interrogation, even if labeled torture, and military commissions, whereas Democrats did not. So the subject was politicized in that sense.

Conclusion

The ICRC has been highly active in trying to protect human dignity through its detention visits (and its tracing activities). In many instances in Iraq and elsewhere, the ICRC is the only actor capable of restoring family contacts and visiting individuals who are detained. In the midst of the US "war on terrorism," the ICRC has persisted in its view that IHL is often applicable and should be respected. In this difficult international environment where even liberal democratic states violate the norms of IHL by holding individuals indefinitely without legal charges, or hiding individuals, or sending detainees to countries known to use torture in interrogation, the ICRC has continued to press for humanitarian protections. It has done so mostly in its traditional, discreet way. In some instances there has been some progress (Gitmo) and in other cases ("black sites") the ICRC continued to be frustrated in its humanitarian efforts until the secret prisons were presumably closed in 2006.

Notes

1 Roundtable discussion, *Jim Lehrer News Hour*, PBS TV, 24 August 2004, transcript, p. 4, http://0-web.lexis-nexis.com.library.unl.edu/universe/docum ent?_m=fdea9b987ef4c59a26.
2 The Hague Conventions of 1899 and 1907 mentioned POWs but provided no regulations for visits. The notion of humane treatment for enemy fighters has a much longer history, going back well beyond 1899. The history of mistreatment of enemy fighters is also quite lengthy.
3 Readers may recall that the Third 1949 GC pertains to combatants, while the Fourth 1949 GC pertains to civilians, both in international war and occupied territory.
4 We use as synonyms internal war, civil war, and non-international armed conflict.
5 In the Spanish violence of the 1930s, the elected republican government, left of center, was challenged by, and eventually replaced by, the rebels led by General Franco, right of center. The Soviet Union actively supported

the republican government, while the fascist governments in Berlin and Rome supported the forces of Franco. Outside involvement in the Spanish hostilities was open and observable, yet the conflict was still considered fundamentally a civil war.

6 This mini-treaty on non-international armed conflict manifests a "material field of application" that is somewhat different from Common Article 3. To simplify, Common Article 3 has broader scope than Protocol II, the former pertaining to all internal wars. The latter pertains to certain internal wars having certain characteristics—the rebel side, for example, is supposed to control territory (how much and for how long is not clear). At least the technicalities of the law suggest this interpretation to legal specialists.

7 This is not the place for extended discussion about which norms of human rights law apply in armed conflict. Suffice it to say that in addition to the UN Convention Against Torture, which applies in peace or war, there is the International Covenant on Civil and Political Rights. The latter treaty contains certain provisions, such as protection of the right to life, which states cannot derogate from, even in times of national emergency threatening the life of the nation. Thus not only does IHL prohibit summary execution and torture, among other acts, in wartime and occupation, but so do certain provisions of international human rights law.

8 See especially *International Review of the Red Cross*, 87, no. 857 (March 2005), special issue on detention.

9 The legal type of conflict affects who might get a copy of the formal report. In international armed conflict, both the detaining state and the state of prisoner's origin get a copy. In other types of conflict, only the detaining party gets a copy. Even for the detaining party, there is some question as to where the report should go—foreign office, military authorities, office of the chief executive, etc. All of this took on renewed importance after 2003 and the question of US mistreatment of prisoners in Iraq. See the subsequent case study, below.

10 See especially "Action by the International Committee of the Red Cross in the Event of Violations of International Humanitarian Law or of other Fundamental Rules Protecting Persons in Situations of Violence," *International Review of the Red Cross*, 87, no. 858 (June 2005), 303–400.

11 "Interview with Lech Walesa," *International Review of the Red Cross*, 87, no. 857 (March 2005), 9–14, at 11.

12 Forsythe, *The Humanitarians*, 294.

13 The points are developed at some length in Forsythe, *The Humanitarians*. See also David P. Forsythe, "The Ethics of ICRC Discretion," *Millennium*, 34, no. 2 (2005), 461–75.

14 ICRC Press Release 06/64, 27 June 2006. Other ICRC press reports at about the same time were not as bold, but reflected the more usual ICRC preference for vague, even handed, non-pointed public statements.

15 Official statement of the ICRC, "The Relevance of IHL in the Context of Terrorism," 21 July 2005, http://www.icrc.org. Several statements by US officials accepted API, Article 75, as customary international law binding on the United States.

16 The best overview of this process is to be found in Karen J. Greenbert and Joshua L. Dratel, eds, *The Torture Papers: The Road to Abu Ghraib* (Cambridge: Cambridge University Press, 2005).

17 There were always those in Washington who saw a role for IHL and other parts of international law during the US "war on terrorism." But they were shut out of the policy-making process, and/or their views were rejected by those wanting an all-powerful executive unconstrained by national and international law and related organizations. See, for example, Jane Mayer, "Letter from Washington: The Hidden Power," *New Yorker*, 3 July 2006, starting at 44.

18 Mark Danner, *Torture and Truth: America, Abu Ghraib, and the War on Terrorism* (New York: New York Review of Books, 2004), 84.

19 Erik Saar and Viveca Novak, *Inside the Wire: A Military Intelligence Soldier's Eyewitness Account of Life at Guantanamo* (New York: Penguin Press, 2005), 161.

20 Among numerous sources, see the clear and correct exposition in Silvia Borelli, "Casting Light on the Legal Black Hole: International Law and Detentions Abroad in the 'War on Terror,'" *International Review of the Red Cross*, 87, no. 857 (March 2005), 39–68.

21 Gabor Rona, "When Is a War not a War?" www.icrc.org/web/eng/siteeng0. nsf/htmlall/5xcmnj?opendocument. Rona at that time was an ICRC lawyer.

22 Gitmo was chosen because it was leased in perpetuity from Cuba, and thus in the hope that US courts would accept the administration's argument that the courts had no jurisdiction there since the United States was not sovereign over that territory. US courts, however, did assert their jurisdiction (see the Rasul case by the US Supreme Court). The choice of Gitmo is yet further evidence that the administration sought a free hand in dealing with "enemy prisoners," unsupervised by national or international authorities.

23 See, for example, Jane Mayer, "Annals of the Pentagon: The Memo," *New Yorker*, 27 February 2006, starting at 32. George Aldrich, who was head of the US delegation to the 1974–77 diplomatic conference that produced API and APII, also disagreed with the legal arguments of the Bush administration denigrating the application of IHL to Afghanistan and to Gitmo. See his book review in the *American Journal of International Law*, 100, no. 2 (April 2006), 495–99.

24 Saar and Novak, *Inside the Wire*, 272.

25 Saar and Novak, *Inside the Wire*, 274.

26 See David P. Forsythe, "United States Policy toward Enemy Detainees in the 'War on Terrorism,'" *Human Rights Quarterly*, 28, no. 2 (May 2006), 465–91.

27 We know about prisoner abuse at Gitmo from a partial ICRC report leaked to the *New York Times*, probably by dissidents within the executive branch; from two books written by US military personnel with access there; from the claims of released prisoners as evaluated by human rights NGOs; from media reports based on interviews with persons who had access to prisoners; and from the defense lawyers assigned to prisoners who were charged before US military commissions (up until mid-2006). On the other hand, the official line from the Bush administration was that all prisoners there were treated humanely.

28 IRF refers to Initial Reaction Force at Gitmo. Saar and Novak, *Inside the Wire*, 102.

29 See further especially Joseph Margulies, *Guantanamo and the Abuse of Presidential Power* (New York: Simon & Schuster, 2006), and Steven H.

Miles, *Oath Betrayed: Torture, Medical Complicity, and the War on Terror* (New York: Random House, 2006).

30 Saar and Novak, *Inside the Wire*, 66.

31 Angela Bennett, *The Geneva Convention: The Hidden Origins of the Red Cross* (Gloucester: Sutton Publishing, 2005), 198.

32 www.nytimes.com/2005/04/20/international/asia/20afghan.html.

33 Associated Press, 17 June 2005, http://0-web.lexisnexis.com.library.unl.edu/universe/documents/_m = c5313ea15785a028d.

34 It is worth mentioning that most of the interrogators at Baghram came to believe that Dilawar was an innocent man who was merely in the wrong place at the wrong time.

35 Various articles detail the extent of the abuse at Baghram. Tim Golden, "Years After 2 Afghans Died, Abuse Case Falters," 13 February 2006, www.nytimes.com/2006/02/13/national/13bagram.html. Douglas Jehl, "Army Details Scale of Abuse of Prisoners in an Afghan Jail," 12 March 2005, www.nytimes.com/2005/03/12/politics/12detain.html. Tim Golden, "In U.S. Report, Brutal Details of Two Afghan Inmates' Deaths," 20 May 2005, www.nytimes.com/2005/05/20/international/asia/20abuse.html.

36 ICRC press release no. 06/43, 12 May 2006.

37 Eric Schmitt, "Abuse Inquiry Finds Flaws," *New York Times*, 4 December 2004.

38 www.hrw.org/english/docs/2005/04/24/usint10511_txt.htm.

39 *New York Times*, 22 January 2006, "Army Interrogator Found Guilty in Iraqi's Death" www.nytimes.com/aponline/national/AP-Iraq-Suffocation.html.

40 Danner, *Torture and Truth*, 251–75. The broad, systematic nature of abuse was also confirmed by several US military reports.

41 See a long case study in Forsythe, *The Humanitarians*. Conventional wisdom holds that the ICRC prison reports about Abu Ghraib in the fall of 2003 should have set off alarm bells in Washington, but they did not. This led to a discussion of where future ICRC reports should be sent.

42 While the Court held in Hamdan v. Rumsfeld (no. 05–184) that 1949 Common Article 3 was relevant to Gitmo detainees, the ICRC more correctly held that the violence in Afghanistan, at least in part, should be legally governed by the IHL for international war, not just internal war.

43 For the critique that the ICRC should have spoken out more about US abuse at Gitmo and elsewhere, see Daniel Warner, "The ICRC and the Public/Private Divide," *Millennium*, 34, no. 2 (2005), 449–60.

6   Conclusion

- **The future of the ICRC**
- **International trends**
- **Relevance of IHL and Red Cross neutrality**
- **Last thoughts**

The future of the ICRC

In earlier chapters we discussed the history and activities of the ICRC. This chapter looks at the future direction of the organization. Specifically, we discuss some of the most pressing issues that the ICRC will have to face in the twenty-first century. We explore the challenges confronting the organization and assess its relevance in contemporary international relations. We conclude by suggesting that the ICRC is still an important actor with a neutral role to play in world affairs.

International trends

Suffice it to say that in international relations or world affairs at the start of the twenty-first century, there is no lack of political conflict. Likewise, there remains a pressing need for attention to humanitarian affairs in these conflicts. Whether one looks at the eastern Mediterranean (the question of Palestine/Israel; Syrian civil war), Afghanistan and Iraq (the US war on terrorism, now including Somalia and Yemen), various parts of Africa where Darfur drags on but South Sudan may be worse, or certain other parts of the globe, one finds deadly conflict and much human suffering—mainly by civilians but also by combatants.

Now it may be that certain long-term trends are encouraging for those concerned with peace and war. A global war has not occurred since 1945, and even lesser forms of combat among states with major military establishments have shown a remarkable decline since the Cold War ended in about 1989.[1] Even the states that have developed nuclear weapons have thus far (since 1945) recognized the dangers of using them—although one cannot be certain that this restraint will continue. (Any large-scale use of nuclear weapons would render obsolete many key provisions of international humanitarian law, such as the distinction between civilian and combatant, or between medical and non-medical facilities.)

Other trends are not so encouraging for those interested in humanitarian values. Increasingly civilians are made the object of intentional attack, either because of ethnic cleansing, or to sow terror, or as collective punishment, or for some other reason. All too often combatants who are *hors de combat* are not given a humanitarian quarantine but rather are abused either for reasons of hatred or in a quest for "actionable intelligence." The Islamic State (ISIS or ISIL) in Iraq and Syria and Boko Haram in northeast Nigeria believe in total war, observing almost no limits on their violent crusades, and consciously engage in atrocities in order to intimidate, deter, and perversely recruit.

Third-party states that do not have vested interests in conflicts are often reluctant to expend blood and treasure to enforce humanitarian restraints. Even in the Darfur region of the Sudan, where either genocide or something approaching genocide occurred over many years, the atrocities dragged on without conclusive response. Likewise, in the Democratic Republic of Congo over a number of years there were more people killed, mostly civilians, than in any other conflict since 1945. Yet the overall response to this enormous human catastrophe was one of disregard and dithering.

Common Article 1 of the 1949 Geneva Conventions requires states "to respect and to ensure respect for the present Convention[s] in all circumstances." But often states observing a conflict do not take on the responsibility to see that the law is properly applied.

It has been said that those who study violations of human rights and humanitarian norms will never lack for subject matter. So it can be said that even with the decline of war among the great powers since 1945,[2] there is no lack of need for the traditional work of the ICRC as it seeks to respond to human suffering in political conflict. More of the world may be encompassed in a democratic peace than ever before,[3] but that peaceful democratic community of consolidated liberal democracies still leaves room for much conflict and human suffering. There are unfortunate reasons explaining why the ICRC budget now runs about $1.4 billion.

Relevance of IHL and Red Cross neutrality

The 1864 GC was developed by states, for states, with a focus on interstate war. In the twenty-first century, threats to the human dignity of soldiers and civilians no longer stem solely—or even primarily—from wars among states. In contemporary times, internal wars of various sorts far outnumber international wars. Often the fighters for a principal party do not wear a uniform and there is often an absence of a clear chain of military command. Most of IHL was not drafted with Al Qaeda or Hezbollah or the Tamil Tigers (Sri Lanka) in mind, much less the Islamic State or Boko Haram or Al Shabab. It is true, however, that 1949 Common Article 3 and also 1977 Additional Protocol II were attempts to deal with irregular fighters and forms of armed conflict different from traditional international war.

Are the Geneva Conventions and the international humanitarian law of which they are a part still relevant today given the realities of world politics? Given the nature of international relations today, can the ICRC seriously protect human dignity, tied as it is to the GCs and Protocols? Do the ICRC and the idea of Red Cross neutrality still have a role to play? We argue that the answer to this is mostly yes. Despite protestations to the contrary by certain parties, most of the values found in IHL remain relevant, even if the ICRC may have a more difficult time identifying the armed individuals or groups to negotiate with.

Despite prevalent American views after 11 September 2001, terrorism is not new, and the world did not fundamentally change because civilians in a democracy were killed by a non-state actor trying to employ mass violence. France faced "terrorists" in Algeria in the 1950s, Britain confronted the Irish Republican Army some decades ago with hidden bombs going off in downtown London, Germany faced the Red Army Faction and other violent groups, and so on. In fact, the British establishment regarded the Americans as terrorists in the 1770s and 1780s for their often irregular forces, lack of uniforms, and ambushes. A Serbian "terrorist" triggered World War I with his assassination of the Archduke of the Austro-Hungarian Empire; he did so on behalf of the Black Hand, a shadowy political organization dedicated to Serb nationalism and opposed to Austro-Hungarian expansion into the western Balkans. And so on. In many ways the "question of terrorism" is but one form of trying to limit, if not erase, those who believe in total war—mainly through the attacking of civilians and civilian objects. This occurs for several reasons: one's cause is seen as totally just, whereas the other side is seen as totally evil; the other side possesses superior conventional power, thus leading to unconventional attacks; civilians are seen as responsible for the power of the political opponent, since civilians either elected the political actors or deferred to the hated policies. Whatever the details, the ICRC and IHL have always taken a position against total war thinking and for legal moral restraints on war fighting. Whether moderation in war is an imbecility or a courageous stand is hardly a new subject.[4]

How one legally regulates and obligates non-state parties is tricky business. IHL, like all of international law, is officially made by states. As far as treaty law is concerned, states have to give their consent, otherwise they are not bound. (The United States, for example, argues that it is not bound by most of the articles found in API and APII from 1977, since Washington has never consented to those legal instruments. The United States only accepts those provisions that have arguably passed into customary international law.) But non-state parties, such as the rebel side in a civil war, or a national liberation movement (assuming one can define such an actor), or a "terrorist" organization, or a private militia is not allowed to sign, ratify, or accede to treaties.

These types of irregular or non-state actors and their fighting forces are said to be obligated under IHL because they seek to be a public actor and undertake violence in a state that is a party to the GCs.

While from a legal point of view this is not an entirely satisfactory reasoning, it is the only way to get to a point where all fighting parties are said to be legally obligated to conduct limited war in a reciprocal relationship. All states are party to the 1949 GCs, and all states therefore formally accept the notion of limited war occurring on their territory (which is not the same as really believing in it).[5] They assert that their non-state enemies are also bound. Whatever the merits of legal logic, the International Criminal Tribunal for the former Yugoslavia has held that individuals, including those from non-state parties, can be charged with war crimes in non-international armed conflict.

As we showed in Chapters 3–5, most governments and their publics accept the notion that the struggle against terrorists and other irregular fighters should be conducted within the limits of IHL. It is not as if the ICRC stood for values that are now formally rejected by the international community. On the other hand, we repeat that formal acceptance of IHL is not the same as seriously implementing it. In 2015 Jeb Bush, running for US president in the Republican party primaries, said he would not rule out waterboarding when dealing with terrorists. Waterboarding is torture.

For the practical work of the ICRC, too much can be made of legal complexities. Frequently the ICRC will distill the legal technicalities of IHL into certain basic principles, and then operate in keeping with those principles. After 1967, Israel detained a number of enemy irregular fighters who perhaps represented some Palestinian militant faction, and/or who might have been a Lebanese or Iranian or Syrian citizen fighting for another non-state actor. The point for the ICRC was to try to secure for these "enemy prisoners" as humane a detention as the situation allowed, regardless of the legal status of the organization sponsoring the violence. The ICRC has pursued humanitarian principles and policies, with some effect, regardless of the complexity and controversies of legal argument.

The "era of terrorism" and much violence by non-state actors give rise to legal complexity, but this does not negate a role for the ICRC in responding to humanitarian need on the basis of RC neutrality. The ICRC has been active in Darfur, Liberia, Sierra Leone, south Lebanon, and all the other violent conflicts even though they were often not classic inter-state wars, and even though they featured much violence by some type of non-state actor. The ICRC found a way to be active in the Syrian civil war, despite the multiplicity of armed actors and the failure of outside major powers to impose limits on the violence or curtail it. It devoted much effort to mitigating the atrocities found in messy situations such as South Sudan, the Central African Republic, Mali, and elsewhere.

Detention visits: the US case study

Not all ICRC detention visits are similar to those conducted in relation to the US "war on terrorism," but that case demonstrates many fundamentals about this phase of ICRC humanitarian protection. With hindsight, what is striking about the arguments of the Bush administration in its "war on terrorism"—namely that IHL did not pertain to anyone at Gitmo, and not to most captured enemy fighters in Afghanistan—is that those arguments did not prevail. As we showed in Chapter 5, the Congress prohibited torture and mistreatment of enemy detainees, and the Supreme Court held that at least GC Common Article 3 from 1949 covered Gitmo detainees. The latter norm from IHL governs criminal proceedings and the interrogation process, among other subjects. Thus, what is striking about Bush's efforts to bypass the obligations of IHL (and of UN human rights standards also), is the negative reaction they eventually produced in Washington (in the context of much criticism from American civil society groups and media organizations, not to mention much criticism from the rest of the world).

Hence, what should be stressed is that a certain type of total war thinking did not prevail (to be sure, despite the determined efforts of the administration) even when dealing with a network like Al Qaeda that believed in total war. Many members of Congress recognized that trying to bypass legal restraints in the "war on terrorism" had cost the United States dearly in terms of status and standing, at home and abroad. This is testimony to the strength of the expectation that fighting parties will respect humanitarian standards. After 9/11, even in an asymmetrical conflict in which the militants obviously attacked civilians, the United States over time returned to IHL standards in its detention policies. This was not the case 2002 to 2006, but it was mostly the case thereafter.

Likewise, when Israel in 2006 responded to the violence of Hezbollah, a terrorist group based in Lebanon, there was much pressure on Israel to conduct its military response in keeping with the terms of IHL, even though its principal target was Hezbollah, a non-state "terrorist" actor which had attacked civilian targets. More or less the same sequence played out with regard to violence in Gaza, both in 2008 and 2014. Israel was pressed to act in keeping with IHL, and Hamas in Gaza was criticized for such policies as firing rockets at civilians in Israel, using human shields, and hiding weapons in civilian facilities.

Now this state of affairs, featuring a broad and persistent commitment to "Geneva," especially pertaining to prisoners, was certainly not produced by the ICRC alone. It was the product of much history plus contemporary activism. Many officials of states, NGOs and IGOs took a stand in favor of IHL and human rights, as did some military lawyers and others. In the United States, some military veterans like Senator John McCain, believing in both military honor and American exceptionalism, led the pushback against early policies of the Bush administration. The ICRC was, however, part of this broad transnational process that eventually had an effect on US detention policy. Of course it took some years for this reaction to develop, and in the meantime numerous prisoners were victimized by various Bush policies. (It is also the case that Al Qaeda and other non-state violent parties continued with their total war, with few prisoners held by them surviving captivity. The Islamic State in the Middle East, led by certain Iraqi Sunnis, was even worse; it's beheading of prisoners made Al Qaeda look moderate.)

On the basis of the type of analysis we provided in Chapter 5, history is likely to judge ICRC efforts, if not always the results, favorably for its role in the US "war on terrorism," as it tried to see IHL upheld and the humane treatment, especially of detainees, respected. One can debate whether the organization should have spoken out more about the brutalities it witnessed in various prisons, but its delegates on the ground certainly showed determined efforts to uphold IHL standards. The ICRC managed to press its case in a low-key manner while maintaining respectful relations with top US officials.

Just as the Bush administration moderated some of its opposition to the International Criminal Court, that government was also compelled to adjust its attempt to bypass the relevance of IHL, particularly to Gitmo and Afghanistan. If the United States had, in fact, treated the individuals detained at Gitmo or in prisons in Iraq (Abu Ghraib) and Afghanistan (Bagram) humanely and within the provisions of the Geneva Conventions, Washington would not have faced so much criticism in the world, would not have lost the high moral ground in its struggle, and, presumably, would not have created so many new terrorists ready to die in order to cause the United States harm. Actually, what the ICRC stood for on humanitarian grounds was also in the long-term national interest of the United States.

Moreover, it is not at all clear that the United States obtained much "actionable intelligence" from its abusive interrogations. There is some evidence that many of the Gitmo detainees had no valuable information to give, and that in at least one instance abusive interrogation produced false information that contributed to the US morass in Iraq.[6] Terrorism and insurgency do certainly create some special problems for the ICRC. Witness, for example, the attack on its Baghdad headquarters in 2003. Previously, even in complicated situations such as the Lebanese civil war, the ICRC knew where to find the leaders of various non-state actors. In general, in Lebanon and similar situations, for example the civil war in Sri Lanka, the ICRC was able to establish a zone of humanitarian space in which to carry out its activities, based on convincing the fighting parties of its neutrality and impartiality and independence. When violence erupted in South Lebanon in 2006, the ICRC had long been dealing with Hezbollah leaders. Both Al Qaeda and the various insurgent factions in Iraq created more difficult challenges, since their location and chain of command were not so clear, and since the ICRC image was not so readily accepted. It seems that a number of radical Islamic factions regarded the ICRC as part of the hated "Christian" West. So at the time of writing, and especially recalling facts pertaining to the Islamic State, Boko Haram and Al Shabab, the ICRC had yet to achieve full acceptance as an independent, neutral, and impartial intermediary with many jihadists (Islamic

holy warriors). Yet it was active on the ground in most conflicts, sometimes moving its base of operations to a neighboring area (e.g., Jordan
re Iraq, and Kenya re Somalia). It had a program of dissemination of
IHL to Hamas fighters in Gaza.

Humanitarian assistance

The ICRC has also continued to play a significant role in providing
relief and assistance to millions of people around the world. Assistance
to those in need includes millions spent in the wake of the tsunami
(December 2004) in Indonesia and Sri Lanka, as well as the 2005
earthquake in Pakistan. The ICRC was involved in these operations
because a natural disaster occurred in a country also characterized by
violent conflict, and where, therefore, the ICRC was already active. For
example, in the first week alone after the 2004 tsunami, the ICRC had
distributed medical supplies (some 1,800 family kits) and provided
emergency food aid to over 6,500 individuals in the Aceh region of
Indonesia.[7] In Sri Lanka, another country severely hit by the tsunami,
the ICRC helped evaluate wounded individuals, delivered emergency
supplies including cooking pots, clothing and medical supplies, and
helped to restore contact between family members separated by the
disaster.[8] The ICRC estimated that it had spent 38.9 million CHF
(Swiss francs), or 31.4 million USD (US dollars), in Indonesia and
33.3 million CHF (26.9 million USD) in Sri Lanka on tsunami-related
activities.[9] While the ICRC was not the only humanitarian agency on
the ground after the tsunami, it did provide substantial assistance to
those in need.

Furthermore, the ICRC had been extensively involved in providing
assistance to civilians in Iraq and Lebanon, to cite just two of many
examples. In Iraq in 2005 the ICRC allocated 48.9 million CHF (39.5
million USD) to assist Iraqi civilians by providing food and medical
services, as well as repairing essential infrastructure including the water
supply and sewage systems.[10] In Lebanon the ICRC has encouraged all
actors to respect IHL and to protect civilians. Furthermore, the ICRC
has provided relief to civilians in Cyprus as well as in Lebanon.
Twenty-four tons of food and emergency aid were distributed to some
4,000 civilians in Tyre, Lebanon on 21 July 2006.[11]

Particular facts naturally change from conflict to conflict, but most
fundamentals, and our analytical points, remain valid. We have referred several times to ICRC involvement in Syria from 2011, which in
2015 was the organization's largest relief operation. In mid-2015, South
Sudan was the second largest.

In the midst of primitive conditions and brutal power struggles, the ICRC started its work in South Sudan as usual with an emphasis on water and sanitation systems. Given much civilian displacement and suffering, it provided food assistance to over a million persons. Through 15 health clinics dispersed widely in the area it did over 5,000 surgeries and helped over 3,000 with rehabilitation services after injury or medical care. It ran a large program providing vaccination for cattle, and seeds and farming tools, once again showing a merger of relief and development efforts. The ICRC's primary partners in South Sudan were the RC Federation and eight national RC societies, all from western developed countries except for Qatar. Three other western RC societies donated directly to the South Sudan Red Cross but had no personnel on the ground. No African RC society was able or willing to help its regional neighbor in its distress. The ICRC-led programs were primarily Western funded, one way or the other.

From these brief examples one can see that not only has the ICRC continued to assist civilians and those in need, but that it has also done so in some of the most challenging places in the world, and done so in the midst of hostilities. This suggests that the ICRC and its activities are still very relevant and unfortunately needed in today's political environment.

These relief operations confirm the material presented particularly in Chapter 4 and in dealing with the case studies of Nigeria, the Balkans, and Somalia. Particularly in conflict situations, but also sometimes during natural disasters in zones of conflict, the ICRC remains one of the world's major relief actors. True, it shares the stage with many other IGOs and NGOs active in relief operations, and of course many of the resources are provided by states and their intergovernmental organizations.

The exact importance of the ICRC varies from case to case, as we have shown (e.g. central in Somalia in the early 1990s; second to the UNHCR in the Balkans in the 1990s; etc.). Frequently the humanitarian need is so great in places like South Sudan or the DRC that the presence of many relief actors is desirable. Then, the question becomes one of proper division of labor and minimizing overlap and duplication. As noted, frequently the ICRC, while maintaining its independence, does reach agreement with the UNHCR, UNICEF, WFP, and others about who does what, where and when. For example, the ICRC agreed with MSF in South Sudan as to which organization would provide what medical services in this or that area.

In the matter of RC relief, there is now much greater cooperation among the ICRC, the Federation, and the national RC societies. One saw this in the violence of the eastern Mediterranean in 2006, as the ICRC coordinated with the Lebanese Red Cross and the Syrian Arab Red Crescent, and also with Magen David Adom in Israel (the latter using the Red Crystal emblem in addition to the Red Star of David, as we explained in Chapter 3). In south Lebanon the ICRC-led Red Cross convoys were the first to reach certain villages where civilians were trapped by the Israeli aerial attacks. President Kellenberger went to both Lebanon and Israel in 2006, and in both places he held meetings with the highest officials to press for greater attention to humanitarian norms and conditions. The same was more or less true for the ICRC in South Sudan from 2013 forward. As already noted, the ICRC and the RC Federation in Geneva coordinated efforts and were supported by about a dozen national RC societies, not to mention the newly minted South Sudan Red Cross. President Peter Maurer traveled to the area to emphasize various ICRC concerns in January 2014, and also took up the subject with important donors at various times.

Discretion

Perhaps the major defining feature of the ICRC, at least in a tactical sense, has been its endorsement of a discreet and cooperative approach to public authorities. This has repeatedly led to controversy.

As we have explained, especially in Chapter 5, the ICRC has, throughout most of its existence, dealt with states in a quiet and discreet manner. Thus, if a state is believed to be violating the Geneva Conventions, torturing individuals detained for political reasons, or treating POWs in an inhumane manner, the ICRC has contacted the relevant public authorities and privately raised concerns. Findings about the conditions of detention, for example, are confidentially discussed with the relevant authorities. Thus, in most cases the ICRC will avoid commenting publicly on violations of the Geneva Conventions or detention conditions. There are plenty of ICRC press releases and press conferences, but sensitive subjects are usually referred to in a general and vague if not opaque way. ICRC officials who speak to the press usually try to do so in a way that does not impede their access to victims and related programs on the ground. The ICRC will "go public" about a country's violations in an explicit way only as a last resort. In order for the ICRC to publicly comment on a situation in a country, such as the detention conditions, there has to have been a serious, repeated violation of IHL, a failure of quiet diplomacy, and it must be established that a public statement is the best option for the victims.

This is in sharp contrast to some NGOs who argue that a public statement can mobilize a country to change its practices—the "mobilization of shame." Amnesty International and Doctors Without Borders, to take but two examples, are more favorably disposed toward the mobilization of shame. The naming and shaming approach tries to encourage public pressure by singling out governments that commit human rights and humanitarian law violations. Is publicity more effective than a discreet approach towards governments in an attempt to encourage cooperation and improve the humanitarian situation of vulnerable individuals? The answer seems to be: it depends.

In some instances a public shaming campaign, such as the criticisms directed toward Putin's Russia for brutal policies in Chechnya, has not resulted in many concrete improvements. However, the public criticism of the French government via a leaked ICRC report with regard to the torture of Algerians, did lead to changes in the French treatment of Algerians. Circulation of unauthorized photos of the 1968 My Lai massacre in Vietnam or the 2003 torture of prisoners at Abu Ghraib prison in Iraq did indeed have a positive and major impact in Washington, but photographs of the 1994 genocide in Rwanda or atrocities in Syria after 2011 did not. The context matters—e.g. whether public and legislative opinion is wary of further foreign involvements.

Given the numerous organizations that engage in humanitarian affairs, having one that maintains discretion while others publicly criticize might not be a bad thing. It is worth noting that an NGO that values public criticisms, such as Doctors Without Borders, had to work under ICRC rules of discretion in Rwanda because it was too dangerous for it to do otherwise. Despite criticisms from others that the ICRC should in fact offer information to the public on the circumstances of detention, for instance, the ICRC has been steadfast in maintaining that access to those detained is most often dependent upon discretion and not public criticisms.

The ICRC argues that confidentiality is necessary to undertake its work on behalf of individuals. If the ICRC were to go public with its findings this would jeopardize access to detainees and accomplishment of its humanitarian work. In the words of the ICRC:

> The neutrality which the ICRC is obliged to observe imposes a very high degree of discretion. In particular, the International Committee does not consider itself able to communicate information received from its own delegates.[12]
>
> The purpose of the ICRC is purely humanitarian and apolitical: the committee must first and foremost do everything it can to relieve

the sufferings of victims of war. To do so, it must adhere scrupulously to a line of conduct enabling it to maintain relationships of trust with parties to a conflict.[13]

Thus, the ICRC argues it is able to achieve improvements in the conditions of detention by engaging in private discussions with state leaders rather than going public with its findings. Last, the ICRC does not want to make some individuals held in detention vulnerable to reprisals by issuing a public report. In general, ICRC discretion has been reasonably well considered, given the sensitivities of public authorities.

Despite that evaluation, whether regarding detention or other matters within its mandate, the ICRC is now more outspoken than in previous times. Still, the organization tries to combine the need to communicate with the press and various publics, with the need to maintain the confidence of governments, the latter naturally preferring discreet dialogue over public criticism of their policies. In Chapter 3 we showed how the ICRC participated in a public campaign to ban antipersonnel land mines, but stayed away from public and explicit criticism of particular governments.

Sometimes it is evident that the ICRC is still searching for just the right balance between public criticism and the discreet dialogue that allows its field operations to be approved by fighting parties. In one sequence of events during 2006, the ICRC publicly implied that Israel's military actions in Gaza were disproportionate and a violation of IHL; it then later backed away from any explicit condemnation of Israel about Gaza and Lebanon, saying it was a humanitarian and not a political organization.[14] The ICRC did publicly object when Israeli forces occupied the premises of the Palestinian Red Crescent in Gaza, but it refused to clearly and publicly condemn Israeli attacks on civilians and civilian resources in Lebanon. Whatever this inconsistency and uncertainty, it was clear that the organization was much more cautious in its public statements than Amnesty International (AI). AI publicly and clearly accused Israel of violations of IHL in its policies in both Lebanon and Gaza during 2006.[15] Of course it was the ICRC and not AI that was trying to deliver relief in the midst of violence in Gaza and Lebanon, which required the fighting parties to refrain from attacking ICRC persons and vehicles. The usual process could also be seen in August 2015 when President Maurer visited the Gaza area to emphasize IHL and the ICRC's practical work. He spoke in general terms about the disregard for IHL and the imbalance between military action and humanitarian concerns. The only specific subject he brought up was the excellent work of the Palestine Red Crescent Society.

Independence and neutrality

There is also the question of the independence and neutrality of the organization. Is the ICRC able to maintain its independence and neutrality in contemporary times? The ICRC is a product of the West, and it emerged within the Christian heritage. Furthermore, at various points in its history, it has been affected by Swiss nationalism, and during the Cold War it was not as neutral as it might have been in places like Korea and Southeast Asia.[16] Given this history, is it possible for the ICRC to be truly neutral and independent in its dealings with various liberal and illiberal actors around the world? Despite the ICRC's origins in the Western world and shared liberal values with many Western democracies, this has not kept the ICRC from challenging these Western states. For example, in the development of the anti-personnel land mine treaty, the ICRC took a position in favor of a total ban on possession and use of these mines that was clearly contrary to the views of the United States, one of its major financial contributors. Furthermore the ICRC has been frank, mostly in a discreet process, when Washington has acted contrary to IHL. So the ICRC has not shied away from criticizing some of its more generous donors. Nor have its largely Western, Christian origins prevented it from operating with consent in the non-West. In fact most of its budget is spent on activities in non-Western regions such as Africa. Generally, when the ICRC is blocked by government action, as when the United States denied it access to disappeared persons held in CIA "black sites," it was not culture or geography that prevented access, much less ignorance about the organization, but rather the national calculation of perceived self-interest. In these cases, the independence or neutrality of the ICRC was not at issue.

It is true, however, as mentioned above, that the ICRC has not been accepted as neutral and independent by the Islamic State and similar non-state violent actors, nor have such actors accepted moral legal limits on violence as compared to total war thinking.

Of course there is the view that neutrality is a form of moral bankruptcy, and that one must show "solidarity" with victims and full blown opposition to "evil doers." But this view is contradicted particularly by ICRC operations in the field, which show, both in relief and detention visits, that a neutral and discreet approach can produce some good. There may be no neutral solutions to the root causes of humanitarian suffering, but short of that, there is indeed a useful role for RC neutrality and the ICRC. There are frustrations in the ICRC approach. As an ICRC official commented, when viewing the organization's limited help to victims in the Balkan wars of the 1990s, which echoed earlier frustrations in earlier violence: "the only thing you can do for them is to make sure they are fed before they are shot."[17] While others address root causes, the ICRC finds much acceptance and respect for its neutral and impartial approach to human misery in conflict situations.

Last thoughts

Clearly the ICRC has had a lasting impact on international humanitarianism. Compared to 1859, when Dunant wandered amidst the wounded at Solferino, there have been significant accomplishments concerning the medical treatment of wounded soldiers. Most modern militaries provide some medical assistance to their personnel, and the medical services of the Western nations are quite exceptional. Furthermore, the ICRC has made a significant contribution to the protection of civilians and prisoners. In fact the ICRC is still one of the primary or major actors in protecting the human dignity of various types of prisoners in various types of conflict situations. The ICRC has also played perhaps the most significant role in the early development of IHL.

The ICRC has made a lasting contribution to the protection of human dignity over the course of its long history. Although it began as a small, amateur organization, it has since developed into a professional organization with operations in all parts of the world. It has continued to expand its concern for victims, from wounded soldiers to POWs to civilians. This long, impressive history of dedication to relieving the suffering of the most vulnerable is one of the reasons why the ICRC is a respected institution in many parts of the world, and will largely continue to be so in the future.

In 2013 a book was published that gave much attention to the ICRC.[18] In this view, the ICRC's push for IHL, as well as the broader human rights movement, was part of Western cultural imperialism. Supposedly a main goal of human rights and humanitarian law, as developed by Western agencies, was to maintain a Western domination of world affairs. In this view, the ICRC and IHL seek to advance an "[i]nternational justice [that] is about real victims only in a secondary sense. It is now almost entirely about *itself*." Henceforth the ICRC would be as much about protecting the sacred symbol [the Red Cross emblem] as the victims of war."[19] Having spent much time in the past with ICRC officials not only in Geneva but also in the field, and having spent more time at headquarters in 2015, our view is that the quoted criticism is very much misguided. What was most impressive about our

2015 discussions with multiple levels of ICRC officials was their dedication to remaining a major humanitarian actor for the purpose of helping victims of political violence. Naturally there was frustration with the brutal actions of almost all fighting parties in Syria and Iraq, not to mention elsewhere, but that awareness had led to new efforts at practical impact—from regional hubs of RC actors to searching for more support from non-Western states. And even as the ICRC continued with determined (and expanding) action on the ground in places like Syria and South Sudan, ICRC officials were hard at work looking ahead on matters such as drones (or unmanned aerial vehicles), automatic (or robotic) weapons, and new forms of armed conflict (e.g., damage done by electronic as opposed to kinetic weapons).

More than 150 years after the ICRC got started and more than 65 years after the adoption of the 1949 Geneva Conventions for victims of war, there was ample reason to be frustrated that human dignity was not better protected in situations of political violence. But one did not find at ICRC headquarters a sense of fatigue with, much less surrender to, brutal power politics so evident in much of the world. What one found, rather, was a commitment to its traditional mandate in order to access victims of political violence in order to improve their lives.

Notes

1 Andrew Mack, ed., *Human Security Report 2005* (Oxford: Oxford University Press, 2005).
2 See further John Mueller, *Quiet Cataclysm: Reflections on the Recent Transformation of World Politics* (New York: HarperCollins, 1995).
3 See Bruce Russett, *Grasping the Democratic Peace: Principles for a Post-Cold War World* (Princeton, N.J.: Princeton University Press, 1993). And Max Singer and Aaron Wildavsky, *The Real World Order* (Chatham, N.J.: Chatham House Publishers, 1996), rev. ed., on how much of the world is made up of peaceful democratic capitalists.
4 See further David P. Forsythe, *The Humanitarians: The International Committee of the Red Cross* (Cambridge: Cambridge University Press, 2005).
5 Some, including some in the security services of liberal democracies, believe that the truly humane approach to war is to fight a total war and thus get the killing and suffering over with as quickly as possible while fully intimidating opponents. Unfortunately for this point of view, pursuit of total war does not guarantee a quick ending, but sometimes only an equally brutal response by the other side. Neither the Nazi bombing of London, nor the Allied bombing of German cities, undermined the will to resist on either side.
6 As of 2006, over 300 Gitmo detainees had been released without charge or trial, because they presented no danger to the United States. Also, a

number of US officials with access to Gitmo detainees stated that there were very few "high value" prisoners there. See Bob Herbert, "The Law Gets a Toehold," *New York Times*, 13 July 2006, A-23. Furthermore, in the case of Ibn al Shaykh al Libbi, it appears that he was the source of the "information" linking Saddam Hussein to Al Qaeda. This link was often cited by Vice President Cheney and others as justifying the US invasion of Iraq. But it appears that this "information" was elicited under torture. Al Libbi supposedly recanted his "testimony." See Brian Ross and Richard Esposito, "CIA's Harsh Interrogation Techniques Described," *ABC News*, 18 November 2005, http://abcnews.go.com/WNT/print?id=1322866. And, "Illegal, Immoral and Pointless," *New York Times*, 10 December 2005, A-28. So, on balance, it is not at all clear that abusive detention is in the national interest.

7 News no. 04/151, 31 December 2004.
8 News no. 04/149, 28 December 2004.
9 Press release no. 05/72, 7 December 2005.
10 Operational update, 31 March 2006.
11 Press release, 21 July 2006.
12 Francois Bugnion, *The International Committee of the Red Cross and the Protection of War Victims* (Geneva, Switzerland: ICRC, 2003), 152.
13 Bugnion, *The International Committee of the Red Cross and the Protection of War Victims*, 152–53.
14 ICRC Press release no. 06/73, 1 July 2006, "Gaza Strip: ICRC Calls for Respect for International Humanitarian Law." But compare the statement by the Director of Operations, Pierre Kraehenbuehl, as reported by Agence France-Presse on 19 July 2006, backing away from any explicit criticism of Israel in public.
15 *AI*, 3 July 2006, "Israel/Occupied Territories: Deliberate Attacks a War Crime."
16 Forsythe, *The Humanitarians*. Urs Boegli, quoted by Elizabeth Becker in "Red Cross Man in Guantanamo: A 'Busybody,' but Not Unwelcome," *New York Times*, 20 February 2002, A-10.
17 Urs Boegli, quoted by Elizabeth Becker in "Red Cross Man in Guantanamo: A 'Busybody,' but Not Unwelcome," *New York Times*, 20 February 2002, A-10.
18 Stephen Hopgood, *The Endtimes of Human Rights*. (Ithaca, NY: Cornell University Press, 2013)
19 Stephen Hopgood, *The Endtimes of Human Rights*, 29 and 37.

Select bibliography

Barnett, Michael. 2011. *Empire of Humanity: A History of Humanitarianism.* Ithaca, NY: Cornell University Press. A broad brush history of humanitarian efforts with much attention to the ICRC.

Best, Geoffrey. 1994. *War and Law Since 1945.* Oxford: Oxford University Press. A highly readable overview of the modern attempt to impose a humanitarian legal order on war.

Blaudendistel, Ranier. 2006. *Between Bombs and Good Intentions: The International Committee of the Red Cross (ICRC) and the Italo-Ethiopian War, 1935–1936.* New York: Berghahn Books. An important book based on much archival research showing how in the 1930s the conservative ICRC tilted toward the Italian fascists at the expense of war victims in Ethiopia.

Bugnion, Francois. 2003. *The International Committee of the Red Cross and the Protection of War Victims.* London: Macmillan. A condensation of the much longer French version, this book by a experienced ICRC official presents an authoritative overview of efforts by the ICRC over time to develop and implement international humanitarian law in armed conflict. Work with political prisoners is excluded.

Crossland, James. 2014. *Britain and the International Committee of the Red Cross 1939–1945.* Houndmills: Palgrave Macmillan. Shows that Britain distrusted ICRC official Burckhardt, in large part because he tried to mediate an end to the war when London sought the Nazi's total defeat. Burckhardt did not restrict himself to strictly humanitarian concerns.

Danner, Mark. 2004. *Torture and Truth: America, Abu Ghraib, and the War on Terrorism.* New York: New York Review of Books. An American journalist shows clearly how the George W. Bush administration tried to erase the international legal framework for dealing with enemy prisoners, so as to allow abusive interrogation. Some material relates to the ICRC and international humanitarian law.

Delorenzi, Simone. 1999. *ICRC Policy since the End of the Cold War.* Geneva, Switzerland: ICRC. A brief monograph, approved by the ICRC, charting various (slight) changes in ICRC policies after the Cold War.

Durand, André. 1981. *The International Committee of the Red Cross.* Geneva, Switzerland: ICRC. A short and official overview of the ICRC, glossing over many controversies.

Favez, Jean-Claude. 1999. *The Red Cross and the Holocaust.* Cambridge: Cambridge University Press. An important book showing how the ICRC failed to pursue not only certain public statements, but more importantly dynamic discreet diplomacy on behalf of German Holocaust victims. The Swiss government, and indeed certain ICRC leaders, pursued the path of appeasing the Nazis, to guarantee the independence and other interests of Switzerland. ICRC independence, neutrality, and impartiality sometimes came second to Swiss nationalism.

Forsythe, David P. 2005. *The Humanitarians: The International Committee of the Red Cross.* Cambridge: Cambridge University Press. An overview of the ICRC, stressing the growing professionalism of the organization. Original information on the policy making process of the organization.

Forsythe, David P. 1977. *Humanitarian Politics: The International Committee of the Red Cross.* Baltimore, Md.: Johns Hopkins University Press. The first analytical overview of the organization by an independent author, concentrating on the policies and policy making of the ICRC rather than international humanitarian law.

Greenbert, Karen and Dratel, Joshua, eds. 2005. *The Torture Papers: The Road to Abu Ghraib.* Cambridge: Cambridge University Press. An exhaustive collection of documents, including material related to the ICRC, showing how the United States prepared for, and then implemented, the policy of abuse of prisoners supposedly related to the US war on terrorism. Some information on the ICRC.

Hoffman, Peter J. and Weiss, Thomas G. 2006. *Sword and Salve: Confronting New Wars and Humanitarian Crises.* Lanham, Md.: Rowman and Littlefield. This book traces the evolution of the international humanitarian system from its inception with the ICRC through the contemporary challenges of "new wars" and "new humanitarianisms."

Hopgood, Stephen. 2013. *The Endtimes of Human Rights.* Ithaca, NY: Cornell University Press. Correctly sees the ICRC as part of a Western and Christian push for humanitarian values, but incorrectly asserts that the ICRC is more interested in its power and status than in helping victims of political violence. Raises questions about the future of international humanitarianism and human rights, based on the argument that the West is in decline.

Hutchinson, John. 1996. *Champions of Charity: War and the Rise of the Red Cross.* Boulder, Colo.: Westview. The late and acerbic Canadian historian takes a critical look at the Red Cross Movement. A good counterpoint to the large number of fawning histories produced by uncritical authors, and one which is especially keen on gender biases.

Ignatieff, Michael. 1999. *The Warrior's Honor: Ethnic War and the Modern Conscience.* London: Vintage. A Canadian author stresses the importance of the notion of military honor for the proper functioning of international humanitarian law. He presents much information on the ICRC in the Balkans in the 1990s, in the context of the absence of precisely that military honor on the part of most Balkan fighting forces.

Junod, Marcel. 1982. *Warrior Without Weapons.* Geneva, Switzerland: ICRC. The personal memoir of an important ICRC delegate who was active in Ethiopia, Spain, and World War II. See also Blaudendistel (above) for a rather critical view of this delegate.

Minear, Larry. 2002. *The Humanitarian Enterprise: Dilemmas and Discoveries.* Bloomfield, Conn.: Kumarian. An overview of international humanitarianism, with some material on the ICRC.

Minear, Larry and Weiss, Thomas G. 1995. *Mercy Under Fire: War and the Global Humanitarian Community.* Boulder, Colo.: Westview. An analytical analysis of international humanitarianism in conflict situations, comparing the ICRC with other humanitarian actors.

Moorehead, Caroline. 1999. *Dunant's Dream: War, Switzerland and the History of the Red Cross.* New York: HarperCollins. A British journalist presents an entertaining overview of the ICRC, the RC Movement, and Switzerland. Extensive research and interviewing leads to a compelling and sometime critical view of her subjects.

Natsios, Andrew. 1997. *U.S. Foreign Policy and the Four Horsemen of the Apocalypse: Humanitarian Relief in Complex Emergencies.* Greenwood, Conn.: Praeger. A former service NGO and US governmental official shows how humanitarian actors exist in a highly politicized world of states and non-state actors. He presents a mostly favorable view of the ICRC compared to the UNHCR, UNICEF, and the World Food Programme among others.

Neff, Stephen C. 2005. *War and the Law of Nations: A General History.* Cambridge: Cambridge University Press. A good overview of both jus ad bellum and jus in bello, or the law on aggression and self-defense, and international humanitarian law. Some information on the ICRC, and many clever analyses.

Rochat, André. 2005. *L'Homme à la Croix.* Vevey, Switzerland: Editions de l'Aire. Highly uneven personal memoir of an ICRC delegate who achieved a number of good things in the Yemen in the 1960s, but many fewer good things when afterwards he became ICRC Delegate General for the Middle East. Not reliable on many asserted facts.

Weiss, Thomas G. 2013. *Humanitarian Business.* Cambridge and Malden, MA: Polity Press. An analytical overview of global humanitarianism, with passing references to the ICRC. Emphasizes competition for "market share" and other features of the humanitarian aid business.

Index

1977 Additional Protocol I 20, 47,
53–7, 60, 92; Article 75: 91, 98,
109; detention visit 92, 93; IHL in
international wars 53
1977 Additional Protocol II 47, 48,
53–7, 114; Article 3/Protocol II
differences 109; IHL in internal in
wars 20, 53
2005 Additional Protocol III 45;
neutral emblem 58–9

Additional Protocols: civil war/
non-international armed conflict
20, 53, 54–5, 56–7, 92, 109, 114;
combatant/non-combatant
distinction 55–6; convergence of
Hague and Geneva law 55, 56;
government self-interest 57;
ICRC 56, 58; methods of combat
56; rejection of 55, 56, 57; success
57; Third World 54; US 55, 56,
115; *see also* 1949 Geneva
Conventions
Ador, Gustave 12–13, 32, 34
Afghanistan 100, 116; Bagram
prison 103, 111, 118 (torture 103);
international/internal war 100,
111; torture 103; *see also* detention
visit and US war on terrorism;
Gitmo
Africa 14, 22
Aldrich, George 110
Algeria 19, 20, 114
American Civil Liberties Union 102,
105

Amnesty International 5, 25–6, 97,
102; mobilization of shame 122,
123; political prisoner 91
Angola 22, 87
API/APII/APIII *see* Additional
Protocols
Appia, Louis 8, 9, 26
ARC (American Red Cross) 9; 2005
Hurricane Katrina 3, 31, 86; 2010
Haiti earthquake 43; assigned dues
to RC Federation 38, 59; Govern-
ing Board 31; League of Red
Cross Societies 25
Argentina 23, 28
armed conflict 6; humanitarian relief
in 26; ICRC's focus 2;
international/non-international
armed conflict distinction 47–8;
NGO 25–6; *see also* civil war/
internal war; war
Asia 22
Augustine, St, 46

the Balkans 2, 14, 66, 78–82; danger
of relief work in the context of
self-serving states 75, 80–1, 82;
Dayton Accords 82; genocide 63,
81, 88; ICRC 67, 69, 72, 120, 125
(core dilemma 80–2; early role
78–80); media 80, 81–2; relief
operation 67, 69, 75, 79, 120; safe
areas 64; Tito, Josip Broz 78; total
war 81; UNHCR 72, 80, 81, 120;
UNPROFOR 80; US 81, 82; violations of international criminal

Routledge Global Institutions Series

2 The UN Secretary-General and Secretariat (2005)
by Leon Gordenker (Princeton University)

1 The United Nations and Human Rights (2005)
A guide for a new era
by Julie A. Mertus (American University)

Books currently under contract include:

The Regional Development Banks
Lending with a regional flavor
by Jonathan R. Strand (University of Nevada)

Millennium Development Goals (MDGs)
For a people-centered development agenda?
by Sakiko Fukada-Parr (The New School)

The Bank for International Settlements
The politics of global financial supervision in the age of high finance
by Kevin Ozgercin (SUNY College at Old Westbury)

International Migration
by Khalid Koser (Geneva Centre for Security Policy)

The International Monetary Fund (2nd edition)
Politics of conditional lending
by James Raymond Vreeland (Georgetown University)

The UN Global Compact
by Catia Gregoratti (Lund University)

Institutions for Women's Rights
*by Charlotte Patton (York College, CUNY) and
Carolyn Stephenson (University of Hawaii)*

International Aid
by Paul Mosley (University of Sheffield)

Coping with Nuclear Weapons
by W. Pal Sidhu

Global Governance and China
The dragon's learning curve
edited by Scott Kennedy (Indiana University)

The Politics of Global Economic Surveillance
by Martin S. Edwards (Seton Hall University)

Mercy and Mercenaries
Humanitarian agencies and private security companies
by Peter Hoffman

Regional Organizations in the Middle East
by James Worrall (University of Leeds)

Reforming the UN Development System
The politics of incrementalism
by Silke Weinlich (Duisburg-Essen University)

The International Criminal Court
The politics and practice of prosecuting atrocity crimes
by Martin Mennecke (University of Copenhagen)

BRICS
*by João Pontes Nogueira (Catholic University, Rio de Janeiro) and
Monica Herz (Catholic University, Rio de Janeiro)*

The European Union (2nd edition)
Clive Archer (Manchester Metropolitan University)

Protecting the Internally Displaced
Rhetoric and reality
Phil Orchard (University of Queensland)

For further information regarding the series, please contact:

Nicola Parkin, Editor, Politics & International Studies
Taylor & Francis
2 Park Square, Milton Park, Abingdon
Oxford OX14 4RN, UK
Nicola.parkin@tandf.co.uk
www.routledge.com